217660

UNIVE

DRI

D0343833

his bool
self se

DC
LAND

The Thames Valley Heritage Walk

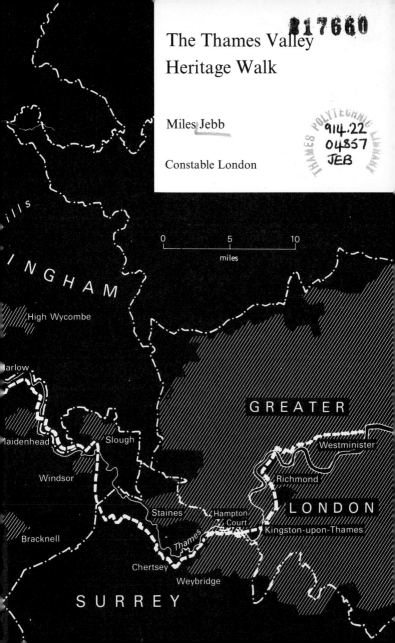

The Thames Valley Heritage Walk

Miles Jebb

Constable London

First published in Great Britain 1980
by Constable & Company Ltd
10 Orange Street London WC2H 7EG
Copyright © 1980 by Miles Jebb
ISBN 0 09 463420 3
Set in Monophoto Times New Roman 9pt
Filmset and printed in Great Britain
by BAS Printers Limited, Over Wallop, Hampshire

Thus sang the uncouth swain to th'oaks and rills,
While the still morn went out with sandals gray,
He touch'd the tender stops of various quills,
With eager thought warbling his Doric lay:
And now the sun had stretch'd out all the hills,
And now was dropt into the western bay;
At last he rose, and twitch'd his mantle blue:
Tomorrow to fresh woods, and pastures new.

Milton, *Lycidas*

Contents

The 32 unattributed photographs were specially taken for this
book by Clive Boursnell

MAPS

The line maps were drawn by Patrick Leeson. The remaining
1 : 100 000 maps are reproduced with the permission of John
Bartholomew & Son Limited

THE CONCEPT

This guide-book is intended for those who like walking not merely
for its own sake, or for a pure enjoyment of nature, but who want to
make use of the pleasure of walking as a means of appreciating our
cultural heritage. My object has been to select a long-distance route
of high quality (and, in particular, nearly all off roads) which has the
maximum historical, literary, and architectural association and
interest: and this has led me to select my 107 miles between
Westminster and Woodstock.

My route differs inherently from the eleven official and various
unofficial long-distance footpaths – or Ways – that exist in England.
In the first place they are throughout established as legal rights of
way, whereas my route passes through several places by permission
and not by right: hence I call my route a Walk and not a Way. In
the second place the official and established Ways are all geared
essentially to geographical features – hills, ridges, coasts, rivers,
moors and forests. My Walk, by contrast, is geared mainly to
architecture – palaces, colleges, churches, old village streets, hamlets,
and even pubs.

Although my route is up the Thames valley, it is by no means a
Thames river walk; and although it is geared to architecture, it is by
no means an urban walk. Of the 107 miles, 31 are along the bank of
the Thames (of which only 2 are beside roads); 18 more are by
public streets or roads (all except 3 in speed-limit zones); 17 are
through parks and gardens; and 41 are on footpaths or bridleways
through the countryside (of which 7 are through woods). So, of the
total 107 miles, only for 20 will walkers be bothered by cars: and
even then, since virtually all these 20 miles are along small streets or
roads with very little traffic, on pavements, and often with high
scenic interest, irritation will be slight. More annoying, I fear, is the
aircraft noise associated with Heathrow, which plagues particularly
Stages 2, 3, 6 and 7; though with the progressive introduction of
quieter aircraft engines this annoyance should through the years
decrease. From the designations of each Stage it can be seen that a

nice balance of the four main elements – river, parks, town and countryside – exists from start to finish, as is apparent from the very outset when one walks out of Whitehall through 3 miles of parks without having to cross a single public road.

In another respect also my route differs from other long-distance walking routes. Because they traverse broad tracts of country, access to them and accommodation along them is often non-existent or, where it exists, usually involves tiresome positioning walks. By contrast, on my route not only are there frequent places where cars can be used for dropping or picking-up, but the public transport – rail, coach and even boat – is so plentiful that it can conveniently be used at the start and end of nearly all my Stages, either by itself or in conjunction with a car. This is a tremendous help towards the avoidance of having to retrace steps and so double one's coverage. Taxis are also everywhere ready at hand, and for three or four people will be hardly more expensive than public transport. (A useful tip for those leaving their cars at one end of their walk: remember that it is much more convenient to take your local transport to the far end and then walk back at leisure towards your car, untroubled by unforeseen delays during your walk.)

As to accommodation, the maximum distance between hotels at any point is 15 miles, and they are supplemented by many guest houses; though the guest houses are less well spread out along the route, and bed-and-breakfast accommodation is generally less readily available than hotel accommodation. Naturally, the hotels vary widely in standards and price: generally, they are of good value and have rooms available at short notice – particularly over the weekend – except during the high holiday periods. Camping presents a problem, especially in the Stages nearest London. But there are 6 public camping sites all within a mile of the route (and a further 1 at Winkfield, 4 miles off-route); and, if 2 sites of the Camping Club of Great Britain – both close to the route – are added, the 8 sites in all provide a sequence which involves a maximum distance between sites of 18 miles in Stages 5–16, quite apart from permission to camp which may be obtained elsewhere locally. In Stages 1–4 the ability to camp does not exist, but the youth hostel at Holland Park halfway through Stage 1 provides an excellent alternative.

The route passes directly by some 70 pubs and close by several

more, and the maximum distance between pubs is only 7 miles. The
first part of Stage 2 is a pub-crawler's paradise, since 10 pubs are
passed in a distance of only 3 miles. Increasingly these pubs serve
food as well as drink, so pub lunches or snacks can conveniently
eliminate the need to carry provisions. Of particular convenience
because of their comparatively remote positions are the Weir public
house near Sunbury Lock in Stage 4, the Fox and Hounds at
Bishopsgate in Stage 6, the Crooked Billet at Stoke Row at the end
of Stage 10, the Perch at Binsey in Stage 15, and the Hand and
Shears at Church Hanborough in Stage 16. A good test of the
quality of a pub is whether it serves real ale (beer which has not
been pressurised), but I have not designated the pubs for this
because of constant changes – generally for the better! Besides
convenient pubs, I have listed restaurants and places for snacks.
Some of the restaurants are extremely expensive, especially in Stages
6–9: of those of good value I particularly recommend Pembroke
Lodge in Stage 3 and the White Hart at Dorchester in Stage 12.

THE STYLE

I have divided the 107 miles into 16 Stages of between $4\frac{1}{2}$ and $8\frac{1}{2}$
miles. These lengths are much shorter than is normal in long-
distance walking guides but are here desirable because of the wealth
of cultural content in virtually every stage. Besides, if the route is
split logistically into short Stages, those who don't consider
themselves as long-distance walkers may be tempted to try a Stage,
especially families who want to walk or stroll through a morning or
afternoon. For them, I have even divided most Stages into
convenient halves, of distances of only 3 miles or so. For stronger
walkers I have specified the public transport over each sequential
four Stages, thus covering the needs of all those who want to walk
up to around 25 miles in a day, which should include nearly
everybody!
    The text is strictly divided between facts about the route and
descriptions about the heritage: the descriptions are not to be used
for route-finding. The only exception is that a number of short
diversions to important places (never over 2 miles) are described in

the general descriptions and not in the actual routes. The route is
written in both directions, because it can in places be complex and
there is no waymarking. All names of roads, streets, lanes, walks,
farms, etc., are stated in the text; and footpath and bridleway signs
are also stated, though these often get damaged, destroyed, or even
stolen. The Bartholomew maps show the outline of each Stage; and
sketch maps are also provided for intricate sections. The use of
Ordnance Survey 1:50 000 series maps for general interest is
suggested: these are sheet 176 for Stages 1–6, sheet 175 for
Stages 6–11, and sheet 164 for Stages 12–16.

I have compromised between imperial and metric by referring to
the longer distances in miles but the shorter ones in metres (which
for our purposes are virtually the same as yards). In the route
headings, kilometres as well as mileages are given, both rounded to
the nearest halves. Elsewhere in the text, miles are to the nearest $\frac{1}{4}$
and metres to the nearest 10 m. Compass bearings are not given
because there are so many distinctive features.

In the Specifics I have throughout avoided quoting prices, because
inflation nowadays makes them inaccurate within a few months! In
public transport details, I have given frequencies and journey-times,
but not schedules which are likewise subject to change. In the
specifics about taxis, accommodation, refreshment and facilities, I
have been selective: often there are other alternatives besides those I
have quoted. So, for example, only a minority of the 70 pubs are
named; and the only public telephones I mention are those in
remote places.

All route descriptions are susceptible to topographic changes after
going into print: but because my route is so closely controlled by
planning restrictions I don't believe there can be any substantial
changes – though the Dorchester bypass will certainly alter the start
of Stage 13. A special word of warning about the designation of the
banks of the Thames and other rivers and waterways: the *left* and
right banks relate to the direction of the flow of the *river*, and the
direction of the *walker* is irrelevant. This time-honoured and
universal rule seems to have been forgotten in some recent walking
guides.

The places at which my route is by permission and not by right
are, firstly, all the parks and gardens. These are usually closed at

night and some are not open till mid-morning, at times as stated. At Kew Gardens and Blenheim Park a small entrance charge is made; and there are various restrictions on dogs, including a total ban in Kew Gardens. Secondly, at two other points we walk by permission: at Sandford, across the premises of the King's Arms; and at Chertsey Mead, where the Elmbridge Borough Council has sanctioned my route in place of the much rougher right of way.

The route is throughout smooth and easy walking, except that at four specified points in Stages 5, 13 and 16 there are boggy patches which need careful negotiation in wet weather, but are all avoidable by detour. In Stages 5, 8, 9, 10, 11, 12, 13 and 16 there are various stiles and occasionally a gate which is locked. These, plus prohibitions in most of the parks and on some of the towpaths, prevent my route from being of interest to bicyclists.

The only hazards are minor ones. Mud is predictable in wet weather, especially in Stages 5, 10, 11, 12, 13 and 16; though Stage 1 is entirely paved and so mud-free. Flooding is rare nowadays, with strict control of Thames water-levels, but on the unusual occasions when it does occur the route could at places become impassable. Cattle will probably be encountered in fields through which the route actually passes in Stages 5, 8, 9, 10, 11, 12, 13, 15 and 16. They will not trouble walkers but will hustle around accompanying dogs: incidentally, farmers are not meant to put aggressive bulls in fields in which are rights of way.

There is no need for me to make any recommendations on footwear, clothing or provisions on a route which is so easy-going and so frequently passing by human habitation. It is an all-weather route, equally enjoyable on a bright winter day (especially with a smattering of snow on the ground) as at any other time. Nor do I presume to suggest how long it takes to walk each Stage. That entirely depends on your disposition and whether you want to stride, walk, or stroll; to stop frequently to savour the new aspects of each turning (and to read my descriptions of them!) or to continue non-stop through several Stages. For those who want to take it fairly slowly, a rule of thumb is to allow an average of $2\frac{1}{2}$ miles to the hour excluding sightseeing – 2 miles if with the family.

To the 107 miles of the route I have added two short extensions. One is through the City of London to the Tower of London. I have not included it in my main route because it is so completely urban and because there are so many associations on or close to it that, if described, would make the book disproportionately weighted towards London. The other is from Woodstock to the Ditchley Gate of Blenheim Park, because this provides a link with the Oxfordshire Way, as well as a further two miles of pleasant walking.

Finally, the text indicates the points at which the route crosses three other long-distance footpaths – the London Countryway, the Oxfordshire Way and the Ridgeway – at points in Stages 6, 8, 10, 11 and Extension B. Besides these, the route at various points co-incides with the Thames Walk, an unofficial long-distance route of 156 miles which keeps as close as possible to the river from Putney (near Hammersmith) to its source.

THE HERITAGE

It is hard to think of anywhere else in the world where over a distance of some 100 miles so many extant cultural and historical treasures are strung out at intervals along the thin thread of a long-distance walking route. This is no accident, but the outcome of a thousand years of the successful development of the English nation-state. No invading armies have marched through London or the Thames Valley since 1066, and the civil war and religious strife of the sixteenth and seventeenth centuries were, by comparison with the rest of northern Europe, relatively mild affairs. Progressive prosperity until very recent times has enriched the route with the glories of art and architecture – a route which neatly avoids the ugly obverse of surrounding industrialisation.

Since historical buildings and landscapes which have survived development and urban blight are preserved more rigorously than ever before, we are able now to enjoy natural and scenic pleasures of more splendour and variety than we would have done had we walked along the route in past centuries, before Kew Gardens or Windsor Great Park existed, or horticulture had enriched the countryside with new species. Particularly I doubt whether any other long-distance walk passes such a fine selection of trees, all the more impressive for not being massed in great woods or forests, but standing alone or in small clumps.

The central natural theme of the route is the Thames – the waterway used by man to develop commerce and purvey culture – and its interplay with surrounding lines of hills, such as the Chilterns and Cotswolds. The central historical theme is the English monarchy, that supremely adaptable institution, and its own interplay with opposing forces – ecclesiastical, baronial, parliamentary and democratic. Most of the 41 monarchs since the Norman conquest find a mention in this book, for their association or influence, beneficent or otherwise, on places along the route. And, in conjunction with these monarchs, the aristocrats who often ruled in their name. The route passes 7 palaces, notably Buckingham Palace, Hampton Court and Blenheim; as well as Windsor Castle and 8 other great houses, notably Apsley House and Chiswick House.

But the heritage of the Thames valley is far more than just a catalogue of princes and their protégés. The streets of Chiswick, Windsor, Eton, Cookham, Henley, Wallingford, Eynsham and Woodstock tell us eloquently of town life in the past 300 years; and the traces of far earlier constructions in the areas of Mongewell, Wittenham and the Baldons give us clues to rural life in previous centuries. Westminster and Oxford, the two poles of the route, confront us with the lengthy traditions of democracy and learning. In and around Whitehall we have many buildings relevant to the British Constitution. In Oxford (and also at Eton) we can observe the beautiful quadrangles and halls of the many colleges in which academic independence flourished. Artistic achievement can be absorbed, not only in the great collections of the National Gallery, Hampton Court, Windsor Castle, the Ashmolean and Blenheim, but also in appreciation of the sites painted by so many famous artists along the route. And literary associations spring to mind at almost every corner, evoking many of our greatest English writers and poets.

Finally, a cathedral, two abbeys and many chapels, as well as the sites of several monasteries, speak to us of the all-pervading influence of Christianity. Besides them, the route passes directly by 25 parish churches and very close to a further 15, giving a string of 40 churches, at least one in every Stage. Most of these churches have some medieval features, and in many of the towns or villages the church is by far the oldest building and the main visual link with the past. In comparison with the rest of the country, and even more so the rest of Northern Europe, these churches are richly furnished with tombs, memorials, pews, pulpits, altars, screens and doors. Particularly notable items are Hogarth's tomb in Chiswick churchyard; the Shannon monument at Walton; the Bonde and Denham brasses at Thorpe; the pews and pulpit at Dorney; the Hoby monuments at Bisham; the Knollys monument at Rotherfield Greys; and the rood screen at Church Hanborough. As entities and examples of very different periods, the churches of greatest impression are perhaps those at Petersham, Thorpe, Cookham, Henley, Iffley, Oxford (St Mary's and St Barnabas'), and Church Hanborough: but any list is inevitably invidious.

Although so much remains, we can hardly be complacent if we consider how much has been destroyed, particularly during the Reformation. Not only was all the glass and most of the statuary smashed, but many of the buildings themselves fell into complete disrepair. Indeed, who can foresee what the state of these present 40 churches will be hundreds of years hence? Clearly, we can no longer take them – or other aspects of our heritage – for granted: they need our active support. As an element in the fabric of our culture they cannot be fully appreciated in merely architectural or artistic terms: for this a spiritual dimension is also needed, and a sympathy, rather than an antipathy, for the successive gradations of Christian worship through the centuries and for the religion which has been so central to our civilisation. So as to emphasise the active life of the churches along the Walk, I have throughout the descriptions referred to them by the name of the saint to whom they are dedicated. It is significant that nearly a quarter are dedicated to the Virgin Mary: in second place comes St Peter, with 5. All except 3 (2 Roman Catholic and 1 Independent Evangelical) are Church of England. Sadly, because of present lawlessness, some of these churches are often closed, but at the time of writing more than half are usually open (in daytime), and of the others the key is usually obtainable.

Floating to our ears across the countryside or through the towns – and mostly unheard by motorists – will come the pure notes of the bells with which these secular and religious buildings are so well endowed, and which comprise an important element in England's musical heritage. These are the harmonious sounds that regulated the lives of ordinary people, and elevated their minds. Their clear contrast to the cacophony of modern amplified music calls to mind the stricture of Plato that changes in musical modes imperceptibly penetrate manners and customs. At all events, they complement the silent architecture along our route, and may also play for us a practical rôle in giving us orientation on a foggy day.

In describing all the scenes along my route I have not hesitated to quote direct from original sources. I have always felt that the selective use of quotations (to 'touch the tender stops of various quills') gives a far more vivid impression than exclusive interpretation. I also hope that my poetic headings will encapsulate the essence of each Stage, and remind walkers of their walks – and talkers of their talks.

THE WALK

I have walked every mile on various occasions, from long sections of over 20 miles to frequent short sections, necessary for detailed checking: seeing them in different seasons, in rain and sun. But I also felt I must cover the entire length of the walk continuously, and this I did during seven days of May, starting from Whitehall on a Saturday morning and reaching Woodstock the following Friday evening.

Being so carefully prepared, the week was entirely uneventful in terms of personal adventure: by contrast, how action-packed in terms of sustained and detailed interest and variety! The scene, the direction, the sights, the associations, were constantly changing, and the exercise of the mind was just as great as that of the legs. This combination of physical effort and concentrated observation made for a full-time absorption, so that there was never a dull moment, even though for some of the days I walked alone – on others being joined by friends. The experience was strengthened by the fact that I stayed throughout along the route and so had no need to use any form of transport from beginning to end. As a result, when I reached Woodstock I felt strangely remote from London, an illusion swiftly shattered when I was whisked back there in a car in two hours or so.

My first night was at the Greyhound Hotel at Hampton Court, where I had a comfortable room and a good meal, although it must be said that the menu was of an extremely standardised type, confined to steak or scampi – day in, day out. The second night, at Great Fosters, was very luxurious, and my room had antique furniture and overlooked the formal garden – all as if in a previous century, especially when dining in the tithe barn, which was almost empty as it was a Sunday. My third night was at Skindles at Maidenhead, though for full comfort I would recommend the Monkey Island Hotel at Bray: I ate at La Riva, by Maidenhead bridge. On the fourth night I came to the Red Lion at Henley, friendly, hospitable and with excellent cuisine; and my window framed a close view of Henley church tower. Then on the fifth night, the George at Wallingford, with all the best features of a comfortable hotel fitted into ancient frame and beams, and around an old courtyard. At Oxford I enjoyed a special privilege, for I stayed as a guest of the Fellows at my old college, and dined with them at the high table in hall. My final few hours into Oxford had been in rain, and I appreciated their hospitality all the more after the discomforts of the afternoon. Thus travellers would have been received in the past – sore from walking or riding, or at the best shaken about in flimsy carriages, often soused with rain, and then revived in the welcoming warmth of the collegiate common-room. And finally, the Bear at Woodstock, that famous hostelry, in whose excellent restaurant I was able to recount my journey to a friend.

What other memories do I have of that full week's walk? Music heard in chapels and churches – Darke in E at Hampton Court Chapel, Stanford in F at Magdalen, and a Bach Fugue at St Mary's, Thorpe – and the chimes of church clocks (which I have listed in an appendix). Glimpses of deer, in Richmond Park, Hampton Court Park, Windsor Great Park, a wood near Rotherfield Greys, and Magdalen grove at Oxford. Yellow flowers of a late spring – buttercups, dandelions, daffodils, cowslips. And mild changes in temperature and climate, gentle winds and intermittent sun, altogether making for good walking weather.

I hope others may do the entire route continuously, whether they stay in hotels, boarding houses, camp sites, youth hostels or indeed ferry to and from their own homes. For those who really want to see

all the sights along the route, as well as walk it – and I am thinking
particularly of visitors from abroad – a fortnight would be an
appropriate time to allow, perhaps stopping for two nights at some
places such as Oxford or Windsor.

The descriptions of each Stage are written in the direction from
Westminster to Woodstock because it is thought that most people
will want to walk out from London rather than in towards it. But
for through-walkers along the entire route, the opposite direction
from Woodstock to Westminster is recommended; partly because it
leads towards a greater concentration of monuments, and partly
because it holds the fractional advantages of having the prevailing
wind and the afternoon sun behind, and is – by 100 metres only –
downhill.

SPECIFICS

Five and a half miles through the West End of London of which 3 are through parks – 4 consecutive royal parks and later Holland Park. Two and a half are on streets, which are all lined with old terrace houses and devoid of heavy traffic. The route is paved throughout. It passes four palaces and several great houses, and at the start at Whitehall is close to many other famous buildings.

ROUTE OUTBOUND

From Horse Guards, Whitehall, to Hammersmith Pier 5½ miles (9·0 km)

(a) From Horse Guards, Whitehall, to Kensington Palace 3 miles (4·5 km)

Under Horse Guards Arch and straight across the parade ground immediately to the left of the Guards Memorial (five figures) and into St James's Park. Straight ahead along the path, passing to the left of the Cake House and then following the lakeside as far as a bridge and for 60 m further. Here take a path up to the right and cross the Mall to enter Stable Yard Road. (If Stable Yard is closed to pedestrians, turn left and then go right into Green Park at the first opportunity.) At Stable Yard turn left in front of Lancaster House to enter Milkmaid's Passage and cross Queen's Walk into Green Park. Take the path which leads ahead just to the right of a large ornamental lamp-post and continue in this direction, past a second lamp-post, to the extremity of Green Park formed by the confluence of Constitution Hill and Piccadilly. Here take pedestrian subways and follow signs for Hyde Park. Cross park carriage road (motor traffic) on to Rotten Row (riding track) and continue to the right of Rotten Row along a parallel bicycle track to its extremity 1 mile on. Cross park Ring Road into Kensington Gardens. Take path to right of a drinking fountain, then left at a fork shortly after, then straight through the Gardens and across the Broad Walk and straight on to a gate set in the wall, with Kensington Palace immediately to the right.

(b) From Kensington Palace to Hammersmith Pier 2½ miles (4·5 km)

From Kensington Gardens cross two private roads (Palace Avenue and Kensington Palace Gardens) and thence by pedestrian passage and York House Place across Kensington Church Street into Holland Street. At extremity, follow Duchess of Bedford Walk and at end by access passage cross Holland Walk into Holland Park. Keeping ruined mansion to the right, enter a colonnade flanked by stone plinths and thence take path leading downhill close to tennis courts, to Abbotsbury Road. After 50 m left, turn right into Oakwood Court, then across Addison Avenue into Addison Crescent. Cross Holland Road by pedestrian crossing, then 100 m right turn left into Russell Gardens. Then right into Elsham Road and left into Addison Gardens and across railway bridge. At end of Addison Gardens, half right into Blythe Road and across Shepherd's Bush Road into Batoum Gardens. Left into Sulgrave Road and right into Trussley Road and under railway arch. Left into Hammersmith Grove. Right into Adie Road and left into Southerton Road. First right into Kilmarsh Road and left into Iffley Road. Right into Glenthorne Road and left into Cambridge Grove and under railway bridge. Right into King Street and left into Macbeth Street and thence by pedestrian subway into Riverside Gardens and to Hammersmith Pier.

ROUTE INBOUND

From Hammersmith Pier to Horse Guards, Whitehall 5½ miles (9·0 km)

(a) From Hammersmith Pier to Kensington Palace 2½ miles (4·5 km)

At Hammersmith Pier walk through Riverside Gardens to pedestrian subway under Great West Road and into Macbeth

Street. Right into King Street and left into Cambridge Grove and under railway bridge. Right into Glenthorne Road and left into Iffley Road. Right into Kilmarsh Road and left into Southerton Road. Right into Adie Road and left into Hammersmith Grove. Right into Trussley Road and under railway arch. Left into Sulgrave Road and right into Batoum Gardens. Across Shepherd's Bush Road into Blythe Road. Half left into Addison Gardens. Just after bridge over railway, right into Elsham Road. Left into Russell Gardens and right into Holland Road. 100 m on, cross Holland Road by pedestrian crossing into Addison Crescent, taking the right-hand curve of the crescent. Across Addison Avenue into Oakwood Court. Left into Abbotsbury Road: 50 m on, right into Holland Park by gate. Take path uphill and enter colonnade. Walk along colonnade and straight ahead through park, keeping to the left of the ruined mansion. Ahead out of park by gate and across Holland Walk slightly left into an access passage leading into Duchess of Bedford Walk. At end, cross Campden Hill Road into Holland Street. Follow Holland Street to extremity. Cross Kensington Church Street and enter York House Place, and thence by pedestrian passage cross two private roads (Kensington Palace Gardens and Palace Avenue) to enter Kensington Gardens by entrance through wall.

(b) From Kensington Palace to Horse Guards, Whitehall 3 miles (4·5 km)

Entering Kensington Gardens by wall entrance from Palace Avenue, follow path straight ahead and across the Broad Walk and on in the same direction to the further end of the Gardens. Cross the park Ring Road and enter Hyde Park by a marked bicycle track running parallel to Rotten Row riding track. At park railings at the end of Rotten Row, turn right to cross the park Carriage Road and thence by steps into Knightsbridge. Here find pedestrian subways and follow signs for Green Park. Take path leading away from roads towards the centre of Green Park, passing by first one and then a second large ornamental lamp-post, to leave the park by crossing Queen's Walk into Milkmaid's Passage and Stable Yard of St James's Palace. (If the precincts of St James's Palace are closed, turn right to the Mall and then left to where Stable Yard Road joins

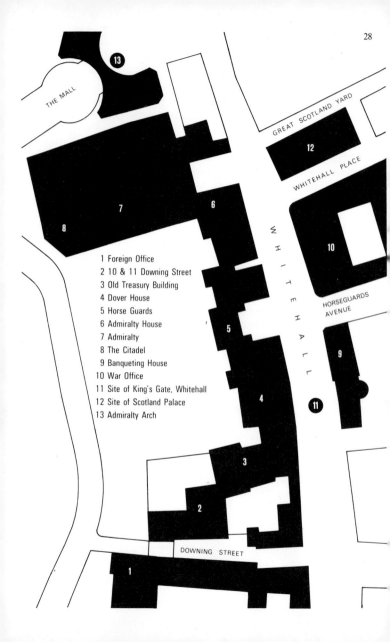

THE MALL

GREAT SCOTLAND YARD

WHITEHALL PLACE

WHITEHALL

HORSEGUARDS AVENUE

DOWNING STREET

1 Foreign Office
2 10 & 11 Downing Street
3 Old Treasury Building
4 Dover House
5 Horse Guards
6 Admiralty House
7 Admiralty
8 The Citadel
9 Banqueting House
10 War Office
11 Site of King's Gate, Whitehall
12 Site of Scotland Palace
13 Admiralty Arch

the Mall.) Right into Stable Yard Road and across the Mall into St James's Park. Take path ahead and slightly left down to the Pond. Follow along the lakeside past bridge and later past the Cake House and emerge on to the Horse Guards parade ground. Walk straight across this and under Horse Guards arch to the gate at Whitehall.

APPROACH BY CAR

Approach Westminster and Kensington are in the heart of the West End of London. Hammersmith is a borough in West London, approached from central London along the Cromwell Road and extensions, and from the west along the M4: from both directions leave the main road at the Hammersmith flyover.

Parking Westminster, Kensington and Hammersmith all have parking meters. Best off-street parking at Westminster is National Car Parks (off Trafalgar Square), and at Hammersmith the King's Mall Car Park in Glenthorne Road.

Taxis Licensed London taxis on the streets.

APPROACH BY PUBLIC TRANSPORT

Trains British Rail stations at Charing Cross and Waterloo ($\frac{1}{4}$ mile and $\frac{1}{2}$ mile respectively from Horse Guards parade). London Transport stations at Westminster and Trafalgar Square (both $\frac{1}{4}$ mile from Horse Guards), Hyde Park Corner, Kensington High Street ($\frac{1}{4}$ mile from Kensington Church Street), and Hammersmith ($\frac{1}{4}$ mile from Hammersmith Pier) **Buses** London Transport at Whitehall, Hyde Park Corner, Kensington Church Street, Shepherd's Bush Road and Glenthorne Road/King Street.

Boats Westminster Pier.

PUBLIC TRANSPORT FROM END OF STAGE 1

To start of Stage 1 Buses from Hammersmith to Trafalgar Square (No. 9 is a through bus running every 10 minutes with journey time

of 25 minutes). London Transport trains from Hammersmith to
Westminster (every 5 minutes with journey time of 15 minutes).

ACCOMMODATION

Hotels Numerous hotels in central London. Of those closest to the
route: the Royal Horseguards Hotel, Whitehall Court, SW1 (01-
730 9191); Royal Garden Hotel, Kensington High Street, W8 (01-
937 8000); and the Cunard International Hotel, Hammersmith, W6
(01–741 1555). **Other hotels and guest houses** Again, a large choice.
Three close to our route are Hotel 128, 128 Holland Road, W14
(01-602 3395); the Miami Hotel, 3 Kensington Court, W8 (01-
937 8248); and the Medway Guest House, 102, Hammersmith
Grove, W6 (01-748 1581). **Youth Hostels** King George VI
Memorial Hostel, Holland House, Holland Walk, London W8 (01-
937 0748), closed November; 38 Bolton Gardens, London SW5 (01-
373 7083); and Kensington Students' Centre, Kensington Church St,
W8 (01-937 5701).

REFRESHMENT

Restaurants The Granby, Whitehall Court; the Serpentine
Restaurant and Cafeteria, Hyde Park; the Belvedere, Holland
Park. **Snacks** The Cake House, St James's Park; cafeteria and
kiosk in Holland Park. **Pubs** The Clarence, Whitehall; the
Coachmakers, Holland Street; the Kensington, Russell Gardens;
the Doves, Hammersmith Pier.

TIMES OF ADMISSION

Parks and Gardens Horse Guards Arch: 06.00–22.00. St James's
Park and Hyde Park: 05.00 to midnight. Green Park: 05.00–22.00
April-October and to 19.00 November-March. Kensington Gardens:
05.00 to dusk. Holland Park: 07.30 to dusk.
Houses and Museums Banqueting House, Whitehall: year-round

daily except Mondays 10.00–17.00 weekdays and 14.00–17.00
Sundays; closed winter bank holidays. Lancaster House: 14.00–18.00
Saturdays and Sundays, and on bank holidays from Easter to mid-
December. Apsley House: year-round daily except Mondays and
Fridays 10.00–18.00 weekdays and 14.30–18.00 Sundays; closed
winter bank holidays and May Day. Kensington Palace: daily,
weekdays from 10.00 and Sundays from 14.00, to 18.00 (March-
September), 17.00 (October and February) and 16.00 (November-
January); closed winter bank holidays.

FACILITIES

Tourist Information British Tourist Authority, 64 St James's Street,
London SW1 (01-629 9191); London Tourist Board, 26 Grosvenor
Gardens, London SW1 (01-730 0791). Note that guard-changing
occurs at 11.30 at Buckingham Palace daily in summer and alternate
days in winter; and at 11.00 weekdays daily and 10.00 Sundays at
Horse Guards. **Toilets** St James's Park (near Horse Guards); Hyde
Park Corner; Kensington Palace Orangery; Holland Park;
Hammersmith Broadway.

DESCRIPTION

Near this my Muse, what most delights her, sees
A living gallery of aged trees;
Bold sons of earth, that thrust their arms so high,
As if once more they would invade the sky.
In such green palaces the first kings reigned,
Slept in their shades, and angels entertained;
With such old counsellors they did advise,
And, by frequenting sacred groves, grew wise.
Free from th'impediments of light and noise,
Man, thus retired, his nobler thoughts employs.

Edmund Waller, 1606–87
from 'Ode on St James's Park'

Two mounted sentries with shining breastplates and plumed helmets
provide a ceremonial start to the Thames Valley Heritage Walk.
Were they to glance to left or right they would see the whole sweep
of Whitehall with those two tall symbols – Big Ben and Nelson – at
either end. The Houses of Parliament, Westminster Abbey, the
National Gallery, St Martin-in-the-Fields, and Downing Street, all
abut on Whitehall, and down the middle of it is a sequence of
equestrian statues leading the eye towards the Cenotaph. But our
two sentries are under orders to look straight ahead, and in so doing
they observe the Banqueting House just across the street: and this,
of all the buildings in Whitehall, has the most relevance to our
Walk. It is all that remains of the Palace of Whitehall – the principal
residence of the English monarchs between 1529 and 1698. The
Banqueting House itself was erected in 1625, designed by Inigo
Jones and decorated inside with ceiling paintings by Rubens. It was
the second piece of architecture in England to be created as a total
entity in the Palladian style (pride of place going to the Queen's
House at Greenwich). From it Charles I stepped to his scaffold on

28 January 1649, and we cannot forget this culminating act as we recall him at various Stages along the Walk, most immediately in St James's Park through which he was led to execution that day, playing out superbly the sacrificial role that he had assigned to himself.

With this sombre reflection, we now start our walk into the courtyard of Horse Guards, an elegant stone building with an octagonal clock tower (built in 1760, to the design of William Kent) and under its arch to emerge on to Horse Guards Parade. Pausing here, just where the Queen reviews the guards in the Birthday Parade in June, we see a series of famous buildings. From the left they are the Foreign Office (George Gilbert Scott, 1873); in front of it, the backs of, respectively, 12, 11 and 10 Downing Street – number 10 being the official residence of the Prime Minister; Old Treasury Building (1736, Kent); Dover House, now the Scottish Office (1758, James Paine) – in which Lord Melbourne, Prime Minister 1834–41, lived as a young man, at the time that his wife Caroline became infatuated with Byron. To the right of Horse Guards arch are next Admiralty House (1788, S. P. Cockerell); the New Admiralty (1895); and the citadel, a bomb-proof bunker (1941). The military nature of the parade-ground is emphasised by a memorial to the five regiments of foot-guards, statues to three field-marshals and, overlooking it from on high, the Duke of York on his column (1834, Benjamin Wyatt).

At the guards' memorial and before entering St James's Park, we should take a parting look at the extraordinary roof-scape of Westminster and Whitehall, and if it is a fine day we can endorse the sentiment of Wordsworth in his sonnet on Westminster Bridge, that 'towers, domes, theatres, and temples lie open unto the fields and to the sky, all bright and glittering in the smokeless air' (smokeless still, now that the banishment of coal from central London has cured the city of its former palls of fog and smog).

St James's Park is the premier of all the London parks, first laid out under Henry VIII, small and exquisite, surrounded by palaces and former palaces. Nowadays, when rulers usually travel in fast cars and with massive escorts, it is refreshing to think that the tradition of walking publicly through St James's Park which was practised regularly by Charles II has been continued by successive

monarchs, prime ministers and foreign secretaries, and recently by
President Carter in 1976. The ducks, geese and pelicans have been
preserved here for over 300 years, and the pelicans descend from
two presented to Charles II by the Russian ambassador. In great
contrast to St James's Park is Green Park: no lake, no flowers, no
adjacent terraces – only the long dull wall along Constitution Hill
(scene of three assassination attempts on Queen Victoria) leading up
one side. But Green Park serves a purpose in being confined to grass
and trees because it prevents the area from becoming too pretty and
too tame.

In between these two parks lie several great houses and palaces.
Looked at from the south side, just before crossing the Mall, and
from the Admiralty Arch end, these are respectively Carlton House
Terrace (Nash), built on the grounds of George IV's former London
residence; Marlborough House (originally 1711, by Wren, later
enlarged by Chambers), built for the Duke and Duchess of
Marlborough, subsequently in royal occupation, and now the
Commonwealth Centre; St James's Palace, the royal palace of the
eighteenth century and still the official palace of the court;
Lancaster House (1827, Benjamin Wyatt), built for the Duke of
York and now a government hospitality centre; and at the end of
the Mall, Buckingham Palace, the monarch's residence in London
since 1837; the façade is 1913 and goes with the Queen Victoria
Memorial in front.

Our route leads across the Mall, whose name derives from the
alley here constructed for Charles II for the game of Pall Mall – an
anglicisation of *Palla a Maglio*, or Ball to Mallet, and a sort of
mixture of bowls, croquet and golf. The Mall has been the scene of
many ceremonial occasions – royal coronations, jubilees, weddings
and funerals, state visits and victory parades – but I like rather to
think of the smaller human incidents, such as when Mozart, as a
boy, was saluted here by George III from his coach: 'The King in
particular threw open the carriage window, put out his head
laughing, and greeted us with head and hands – particularly our
young Master Wolfgang.' We then pass between Clarence House
(part of St James's Palace) and Lancaster House; and before turning

Canaletto: Old Horse Guards Parade

left into the Green Park we can peep into Ambassadors' Court, one of the inner courtyards of St James's Palace. Here the Guards perform their initial and concluding drills before and after the main ceremony in front of Buckingham Palace, and the impression of long tradition is much more effective in this intimate courtyard than in the Edwardian forecourt so familiar to all the world.

The next complex of buildings is at Hyde Park Corner, and is primarily associated with the Duke of Wellington and all things military, though fortunately Hyde Park Corner has not generally become known as Duke of Wellington Place any more than the Étoile in Paris is known as Place Charles de Gaulle. The Wellington Arch (1828, Burton) is surmounted by Peace in her Quadriga (1912, Adrian Jones). In the green below is the Iron Duke himself mounted on his horse Copenhagen (1888, Boehm), facing Apsley House which now contains the Wellington Museum, and flanked by army memorials. The military theme extends beyond the decorative stone screen (Burton) into Hyde Park, where are to be found Achilles (1822, Westmacott), St George, and indeed Byron – whom we can also classify as a military figure, if an unconventional one.

The Wellington Museum contains china, sculpture and paintings belonging to the great duke, principally those presented to him by the King of Spain and the Regent of Portugal. It is appropriate that this Heritage Walk thus starts with full association with one of England's two grandest generals and ends – 106 miles on – with the other, Marlborough. Wellington's individuality is exemplified by his phrase 'I always walk alone', by which he meant he did not share his aims and ambitions with others: but he was not too aloof to escort elegant ladies for walks in Hyde Park. Before leaving Hyde Park Corner we should also note the (present) St George's Hospital, a worthy counterpart to Apsley House; and, as a footnote (or backnote), back-packers may like to know that a porter's rest has been preserved on the pavement of Piccadilly by Green Park just 100 m east of Hyde Park Corner.

And so into Hyde Park and Rotten Row ('*Route du Roi*') where for a full mile walkers compete directly with horsemen, cyclists and joggers, and can observe footballers, and rowers and swimmers in the Serpentine. Energy has now replaced elegance in the use of Hyde Park, where formerly the upper classes would parade in their elaborate clothes, especially during the social season in early summer. But energy and elegance are still combined in the finery and deportment of the Household Cavalry, whose modern barracks are on our left (1970, Spence). The tower block of these barracks and the Hilton Hotel in Park Lane are two disproportionate eyesores which we must try to ignore; and instead we should try to discern, at the lowest point of Rotten Row, the stucco façade of the French Embassy at Albert Gate, and Epstein's sculpture 'Pan' by the Edinburgh Gate, both to our left.

Across the central ring road we enter Kensington Gardens, and pass through a fine grove of plane trees: these magnificent trees were introduced into England in the eighteenth century (and so were unknown to Edmund Waller) and they thrive on London clay. Where we cross an avenue we see to the right an impressive bronze equestrian statue appropriately of Physical Energy (1903, G. F. Watts): to the left, the Albert Memorial (1872, G. G. Scott) and beyond it, the Royal Albert Hall (1871), home of the promenade concerts and other varied events. The Prince Consort is shown as holding in his hand the catalogue of the Great Exhibition of 1851; but sadly Paxton's revolutionary iron and glass exhibition building known as the Crystal Palace, which stood in Hyde Park just in front of the barracks, exists no more.

Through the trees ahead we now can see Kensington Palace, on which all these avenues are aligned, preceded by the round pond, underscored by the broad walk, and secluded behind hawthorn and holly. It was acquired by William III and the east and south sides which we see were designed by Christopher Wren in 1690–6, whilst the gardens were laid out in the 1730s under George II and Queen Caroline, who spent the summer months here, wintering at St James's Palace. Later it was the home of the Duchess of Kent and her daughter Princess Victoria until the daughter's accession as Queen in 1837: various royal personages now use it. There are statues of Queen Victoria (sculpted by her daughter, Princess Louise) and of William III (presented by the Emperor Wilhelm II of Germany) in front of the palace. The whole sequence of these four royal parks certainly stems from royal protection from speculators: but that royalty was not always democratic in its view of the parks is exemplified in Queen Caroline's asking Sir Robert Walpole what

it would cost to enclose St James's Park and restrict public entry. 'Only a crown, madam,' he replied.

On leaving the royal parks we next cross Kensington Palace Gardens. Being a private road and with enormous private houses this has always been the most exclusive of London streets, and for this reason is now almost entirely occupied by embassies, whose seclusion is even greater thanks to a splendid avenue of planes. At Kensington Church Street we for the first time enter the town. This is Kensington, mainly known as a fashionable residential area. Holland Street has several eighteenth-century houses, and flourished when the court was at Kensington Palace. Plaques mark the homes of Walter Crane (1845–1915, artist) and Charles Stanford (1856–1914, musician). Three pedestrian passages and a mews lead to the left. Church Walk leads down to St Mary Abbots Church (1872, Gilbert Scott): it boasts the tallest church spire in London, and the nave gives a great sense of space, but somehow the Victorian medieval has not here succeeded. Gordon Place is a fine example of how to restrict motor traffic in a small terraced street. Later, Holland Street passes the new Kensington and Chelsea Town Hall (1976, Spence), an exciting building faced with bright red brick.

All the part of Kensington which we traverse was once in the estate of Holland House, a great Jacobean mansion, now a ruin, destroyed by incendiary bombs in 1941. Principally it is remembered for the time when it was owned by the third Lord Holland and his dynamic wife who made in it not only a leading centre of the Whig aristocracy but also a literary and artistic salon to which most of the famous names of the period were invited. Macaulay, who was of the inner circle, prophetically wrote, 'In what language shall we speak of that house, once celebrated for its rare attractions to the furthest ends of the civilised world, and now silent and desolate as the grave?' Poignant also is the couplet composed by Lord Holland in recollection of the poet Rogers, which appears as an inscription over a garden seat:

Here Rogers sat, and here forever dwell
With me those pleasures that he sings so well.

South front of Kensington Palace

Meanwhile, Holland Park thrives with mixed activity – a cricket pitch and tennis courts, a children's adventure playground, concerts in the orangery, a restaurant, and a superbly sited youth hostel in what remains of the house.

From Holland Park our object in Stage 1 is to reach the river, and this is done by taking a series of quiet terraced streets to zigzag through the remainder of Kensington and then through to Hammersmith. These streets become progressively down-market as we move westwards, but not necessarily less attractive. The anaemic Abbotsbury Road and heavy Oakwood Court are visually less appealing than, for example, the relatively humble Batoum Gardens or Southerton Road. And Addison Gardens has nice colourful brick houses of the 1880s. With luck, these streets will suffer no further inner-urban decay, and become progressively better looked after. The present revulsion against wholesale destruction of old buildings will serve to preserve most of them.

In Kensington, a deviation of 200 m left along Abbotsbury Road would reach Melbury Road, where lived several late nineteenth century artists, including G. F. Watts and Holman Hunt, and some of the houses are by Norman Shaw: in Holland Park Road, the street just beyond, is Leighton House, with its beautiful Arab hall. In Hammersmith, the route passes by the Godolphin and Latymer School, now a girls' school, but formerly for boys and attended by W. B. Yeats, and by the rather gloomy church of St John (1856, Butterfield) in Glenthorne Road: its gloom may be due to the instruction to Butterfield to make it as cheaply as possible. Our gloom, anyway, will be lifted when after the Great West Road underpass, we reach the end of the Stage at the Thames embankment.

SPECIFICS

The first half of this Stage begins and ends along delightful riverside
terraces which are mostly pedestrian precincts, and in between it
passes through the park of Chiswick House. The second half is in
apparent countryside, and leads first through Kew Gardens and
then along the river bank, beginning and ending by village greens.
Of the whole Stage, only 1 mile is on streets, and the route is
mostly paved, except for sections of the park and the river bank,
where it is on firm gravel.

ROUTE OUTBOUND

From Hammersmith Pier to Richmond Bridge 6 miles (10 km)

(a) From Hammersmith Pier to Kew Bridge 3 miles (4·5 km)
From Hammersmith Pier, always keeping as close as possible to the
left bank of the Thames (the right bank as you look upstream),
follow the path upstream out of Riverside Gardens into Upper
Mall, and thence into Hammersmith Terrace and Chiswick Mall. At
end leave the river up Church Street, then left into Powells Walk
just past the church. At end turn leftwards into Burlington Lane and
cross it by a pedestrian crossing; then 30 m on turn right into
Chiswick Park at Corney Gate. Then take lefthand path for 200 m:
near the Burlington Gate, turn right and walk up to Chiswick House
and round to the left of it on to a path beside a formal garden
with statuary. Where this path divides, take the path half left down
to cross the lake by a bridge. Then straight ahead to the Stavely
Gate and right into Stavely Road. Across Sutton Court Road into
Fauconberg Road. Left into Grove Park Terrace and across
railway. Right into Riverview Grove and left into Riverview Road.
Right into Grove Park Road and then immediately leave it for the
pedestrian riverside path of Strand-on-the-Green. At end, up stairs
to cross the Thames on the downstream side of Kew Bridge.

(b) From Kew Bridge to Richmond Bridge 3 miles (5·5 km)
From Kew Bridge pass to the right bank of the Thames (left as you look upstream) and turn right into Kew Green. Walk along the side of the Green and enter Kew Gardens by the Main Gate. Ahead along the Broad Walk to a monumental urn, left past the Orangery, and then keep on paths always right (except to the tea bar) to find the Brentford Gate. (If Kew Gardens are closed, or you don't want to go through them, turn right from Kew Green into Ferry Lane and left on to the Thames towpath.) Left on to the Thames towpath and continue on it for the remainder of the Stage, past Twickenham Lock and under the Twickenham bridge and railway bridge, after which the towpath becomes Cholmondeley Walk, and up to Richmond Bridge.

ROUTE INBOUND

From Richmond Bridge to Hammersmith Pier 6 miles (10 km)

(a) From Richmond Bridge to Kew Bridge 3 miles (5·5 km)
At Richmond Bridge follow the right bank of the Thames downstream. This leads along Cholmondeley Walk and under the railway bridge and Twickenham bridge, and past Twickenham Lock. Continue along the bank of the Thames for a further two miles until arriving at a car park. Here turn right into the Brentford Gate of Kew Gardens. Follow paths round to the left to reach the Orangery and thence beyond to leave Kew Gardens by the Main Gate. (If Kew Gardens are closed, or you don't want to go through them, continue along the Thames towpath and take the first turning right – Ferry Lane – to arrive at Kew Green.) Walk along the lefthand side of Kew Green. Then cross main road and turn left to cross Thames by Kew Bridge.

(b) From Kew Bridge to Hammersmith Pier 3 miles (4·5 km)
At Kew Bridge take the left bank of the Thames downstream: this soon becomes the riverside path of Strand-on-the-Green. Under the railway bridge and on to the end and into Grove Park Road ahead. A few metres on, turn left into Riverview Road, and then right into

Riverview Grove. Left into Grove Park Terrace and across the railway. Right into Fauconberg Road and across Sutton Court Road into Stavely Road. Left off Stavely Road by Stavely Gate (set between houses) into Chiswick Park. Take path ahead which leads across bridge over lake; then right up path to reach a formal garden with statuary and so to Chiswick House. Pass round to the right of the house and on to just before the Burlington Gate: without leaving the park, take a path left for 200 m to leave the park at Corney Gate. Turn left into Burlington Lane, then cross it by a pedestrian crossing. Then on, to find Powells Walk shortly on the right. Along Powells Walk and to the left of Chiswick church into Church Street, and then right to regain the river bank and walk downstream along Chiswick Mall. Always keeping as close as possible to the river, proceed by Hammersmith Terrace into Upper Mall and thence into Riverside Gardens to Hammersmith Pier.

APPROACH BY CAR

Approach Hammersmith is a borough in West London, approached from central London along the Cromwell Road and extensions. Kew and Richmond are boroughs in Surrey and within Greater London: Kew off the A4, Richmond off the A316 leading to the M3. **Parking** Hammersmith, Kew and Richmond all have parking meters. Best off-street parking at Hammersmith is the King's Mall Car Park in Glenthorne Road; at Kew, Kew Green or Brentford Gate; and at Richmond, the multi-storey car park in the Quadrant. **Taxis** Licensed London taxis on the streets of Hammersmith and Richmond.

APPROACH BY PUBLIC TRANSPORT

Trains London Transport stations at Hammersmith ($\frac{1}{4}$ mile from Hammersmith Pier); Kew Bridge, Kew ($\frac{1}{2}$ mile from Kew Green); and London Transport and British Rail stations at Richmond ($\frac{1}{2}$ mile from Richmond Bridge). **Buses** London Transport at Hammersmith, Kew Bridge and Richmond. **Boats** Kew and Richmond.

PUBLIC TRANSPORT FROM END OF STAGE 2

To start of Stage 2 London Transport trains from Richmond to Hammersmith (every 10 minutes with journey time of 10 minutes). **To start of Stage 1** London Transport trains from Richmond to Westminster (every 20 minutes with journey time of 25 minutes).

ACCOMMODATION

Hotels For Hammersmith, see Stage 1. In Richmond, Quinns Hotel, Sheen Road (01-940 5444); Richmond Gate Hotel, Richmond Hill (01-940 0061); and Star and Garter Hotel, Petersham Road (01-940 5451). **Guest houses and small hotels** Clayton Guest House, 337 Sandycombe Road, Kew Gardens, Richmond (01-948 2902); Spa House Hotel, 52 Richmond Hill, Richmond (01-940 4909).

REFRESHMENT

Restaurant The Cricketers, Richmond Green. **Snacks** Kew Gardens. **Pubs** The Doves, Hammersmith Pier; the City Barge, Strand-on-the-Green; the White Cross, Richmond.

TIMES OF ADMISSION

Parks and Gardens Chiswick Park: daylight hours. Kew Gardens: 10.00 to dusk: no dogs. Syon Park Gardens: daily 10.00–18.00 (to dusk in winter) and closed over Christmas holiday. **Houses and Museums** Chiswick House: daily 08.30–19.00 May to September, 09.30–17.30 March, April and October, and 09.30–16.00 November-February; closed every day 13.00–14.00 and on Mondays and Tuesdays October to March, also on winter bank holidays and Good Friday. Kew Palace: April to October 11.00–17.30 weekdays and 14.00–18.00 Sundays.

FACILITIES

Tourist information Old Richmond Town Hall, Hill Street, Richmond (01-892 0032).
Toilets Hammersmith Broadway; Chiswick Park; Kew Gardens; Richmond.

DESCRIPTION

On the way to Kew
By the river old and gray,
Where in the Long Ago
We laughed and loitered so,
I met a ghost today,
A ghost that told of you,
A ghost of low replies
And sweet inscrutable eyes,
Coming up from Richmond,
As you used to do.

W. E. Henley, 1849–1903
from 'Life and Death'

At Hammersmith Pier the Thames can be seen sweeping past in a great loop and flowing under the brightly painted iron of Hammersmith Bridge (1884, J. Bazalgette). Up this loop come the Oxford and Cambridge crews in their annual boat race in March or April, and a large number of other crews in the more exciting Head of the River race. More ordinarily, there is a lot of barge traffic on these tidal reaches, though none now stops at Hammersmith since the little harbour, or creek, was cleared away in the 1930s.

The first mile of this Stage is along a series of riverside terraces of great charm and variety. The sequence starts in Upper Mall first with Sussex House (1726) and a row of old cottages including the Doves public house, and then Kelmscott House (1780s). This was for eighteen years the home of William Morris (1834–96): in this and adjacent buildings he installed a tapestry loom and a printing press, wrote poetry and preached socialism. He called it Kelmscott House because that was the name of his earlier house far up the Thames, near Lechlade; and once he rowed with his family all the way up the river to it in a small houseboat named 'The Ark'. Preceding him in the house was George MacDonald (1824–1905) who here wrote several of his poems and books, so perceptive of childhood imagination. In Upper Mall, Rivercourt House and Linden House are also good, and in an earlier house on this site Catherine of Braganza, Charles II's queen, lived as a widow 1685–92. We then pass the waterfront of the Latymer school, which faces St Paul's school across the river.

In Hammersmith Terrace, among notable residents were the painter de Loutherbourg (1740–1812) at No 7–8, and at No 13 A. P. Herbert (1890–1971), though two plaques on the houses are not to these but to men of less renown. Herbert was a wit and a supreme individualist, and most appropriately the last Member of Parliament for the University of Oxford. And so into Chiswick Mall, where the river becomes unembanked and in consequence protection from flood-water is an individual affair, with walls and floodgates of varying conviction. The Mall itself is occasionally impassable at very high tide, in which case a short deviation would be necessary. Another consequence of the absence of embankments is that at Chiswick Mall is the first of the Thames islets, or eyots, accumulations of silt with thick vegetation.

The houses in Chiswick Mall are remarkably different from each other. Eighteenth-century houses to watch for are Swan House, Morton House, Strawberry House, and further on, Thames View, Linyard House, Eynham House, Bedford House and Woodroffe House. Walpole House was once a boys' school, and attended by Thackeray: and in *Vanity Fair* he made it the model for the opening scene. The very first sentence of that 'novel without a hero' reads: 'While the present century was in its teens, and on one sun-shiny morning in June, there drove up to the great iron gate of Miss Pinkerton's academy for young ladies, on Chiswick Mall, a large family coach, with two fat horses in blazing harness, driven by a fat coachman in a three-cornered hat and wig, at the rate of four miles an hour.' From it, shortly afterwards, the ruthless Becky Sharp performed the heroical act of throwing the copy of Dr Johnson's dictionary which had just been given her as a parting present into the front garden, in the face of the assembled school.

St Nicholas's church is nineteenth-century but with a fifteenth-century tower, and in the churchyard by the south porch is a

memorial to William Hogarth with an epitaph by Garrick. Also buried here are James MacNeill Whistler, de Loutherbourg, William Kent, and (formerly) the Duchess of Cleveland, the powerful mistress of Charles II. Church Street is charming: in 1765–6 J. J. Rousseau lodged with a grocer in Chiswick, probably in Church Street.

Chiswick House is an architectural triumph, devised by Lord Burlington (the owner) and William Kent and completed by 1730. Their aim was to emulate Palladio's Villa Rotunda at Vicenza, but they also incorporated un-Palladian features such as the spectacular external staircases and the modified internal symmetry. The gardens, as originally laid out by Bridgeman and Kent, were equally triumphant as the first expression of the English Picturesque style of landscape gardening: and although they have suffered much deterioration from their original appearance, we can still get a strong impression of contrived beauty as we proceed past the house and along the line of statuary, then into the wilderness and past the newly restored Ionic temple, and thence across the lake by the ornamental bridge (1788, James Wyatt). In Chiswick Park a deviation from the route by way of Duke's Avenue Gate will bring one to Hogarth House, where the artist lived from 1749 to 1764, antagonistic to his aristocratic neighbour and his Italianate tastes.

Chiswick House was not designed as a residence; it was a Villa attached to an earlier Chiswick House, and later had wings added to it by J. Wyatt: all these have now been demolished. It passed into the Cavendish family and so became a centre of great brilliance, especially under the fifth Duke of Devonshire and his wife Georgina. Charles James Fox and George Canning both died here. Subsequently it was leased to Edward VII when Prince of Wales.

From Chiswick Park to the Thames we traverse half a mile of residential Chiswick. Stavely Road and Sutton Court Road are uninspiring, but Grove Park Terrace becomes progressively attractive. In it is preserved part of a brick ice-house from the former grounds of Sutton House. And so to Strand-on-the-Green, less grand but more intimate than Chiswick Mall. It was originally a group of riverside cottages associated with the ferry, before the

Chiswick House

original Kew bridge was built in 1759. It twice nearly touched national history: Cromwell narrowly escaped arrest when at the Bull's Head and a group of Catholics planned to ambush William III in the narrow country lane behind the village by Turnham Green. The City Barge pub has its origins in the fifteenth century, when a Lord Mayor's Barge was laid up here. Strand-on-the-Green expanded at the time the court was at Kew. John Zoffany lived at what is now called Zoffany House from 1780 to 1810. Nos 64–8 date from 1704, No 68 being particularly charming, with a passion-flower at present covering the wall.

Kew Bridge crosses the silent Thames, but the roar of heavy traffic makes it more like the crossing of some dangerous mountain torrent: we regain tranquillity on Kew Green. We are now in the county of Surrey, and remain in it (except for a short incursion into Middlesex around Hampton Court) till the middle of Stage 6. Kew must be understood firstly in terms of the early Hanoverian kings who acquired country houses here for summer retreat from London, in preference to the palatial alternatives at Hampton or Windsor. They came here for convenience and also for the hunting in Richmond Park: the simplicity of their domestic style can be seen from Kew Palace, formerly known as the Dutch House – because built in 1631 to a Dutch design and with bricks laid in 'Flemish bond' (with sides and end alternating) – which we can see to our right as we pass through Kew Gardens. Here, and also in the now demolished White House, lived George III and his numerous family. Kew Green was where the courtiers and other functionaries lived: how much more agreeable for them than their contemporaries at Versailles who were crowded in anonymous rooms in the vast palace itself! Indeed, this distinction between the English and the Continental styles has been perpetuated ever since: apartment buildings and tower blocks are far more prevalent in the suburbs of Paris than of London; and Greater London, though an ugly sprawl when seen from the air, is punctuated by hundreds of thousands of little gardens.

In Kew Green, then, we pass on the north side a long group of eighteenth-century houses, No 71 being the finest: and across the

Low tide at Strand-on-the-Green

green we can see further variety, including the Royal Cottage. In the
green itself stands St Anne's church (18th and 19th centuries); the
painters Thomas Gainsborough (1727–88) and John Zoffany
(1733–1810) are both buried there.

But Kew's main fame is the Royal Botanic Garden. Born of royal
and aristocratic enthusiasm (Princess Augusta and Lord Bute) and
cherished by early professionalism (Sir Joseph Banks and Sir
William Hooker) it grew to become the best-known botanical
garden in the world. The Garden acts as a centre for the accurate
identification and worldwide distribution of plants, and as a
quarantine station. In the buildings to the right of the main gate
before we enter it are the Herbarium – one of the largest collections
of dried and pressed plants in the world – and the Library. Kew is
increasingly involved in conservation and protection of plants
threatened by extinction.

Our route goes past the Orangery (1761, Chambers), which
houses a permanent exhibition of the botanical activity of Kew, then
across a lawn covered with daffodils in the spring and under birches
and then poplars. A short deviation left would lead to the Palm
House, an immense structure of 1848, by Richard Turner as
engineer and Decimus Burton as architect: Pevsner rates it as more
interesting than the Crystal Palace ever was. And then, further into
Kew Gardens, the Temperate House and various museums, as well
as Temples and a Pagoda – these also designed by William
Chambers.

On returning to the river, averting our eyes from the Brentford
high-rise towers and gas works, but noting the entrance to the
Grand Union Canal – but recalling that Brentford was the nearest
that the Royalists got to London in the Civil War, when Prince
Rupert occupied it on the night of 12 November 1642 – we proceed
up an entirely rural reach of the Thames, with the opposite side
unembanked and with thick bushes, looking much the same as in
Richard Wilson's painting. Very soon a magnificent sight appears:
Syon House, sturdy and honey-coloured, crenellated and turreted
(sixteenth-century with nineteenth-century refacing and with
eighteenth-century interiors by Robert Adam). Formerly a Brigettine

Richard Wilson: Syon House from Richmond Gardens

nunnery, it passed into the possession of Protector Somerset who from it attempted unsuccessfully to launch Lady Jane Grey as Queen in 1553. From him it went to the Earls and Dukes of Northumberland.

Later a second set piece comes into view across the water. This is the village of Isleworth, flanked by Syon Pavilion, a gorgeous Georgian boathouse. Of the old church at Isleworth only the tower remains: the rest of it was set on fire in 1943, not by enemy action, but by local incendiarists. The pub, the London Apprentice, gets its name from the London apprentices' former practice of rowing up to Isleworth in the summer.

Meanwhile on the near side, Kew Gardens has given way to a golf course, in which can be seen the Observatory (1769, Chambers) put here by George III on the site of the former royal residence, Richmond Lodge. Three obelisks (1778, W. Anderson) close to the towpath were placed as meridian marks. Past Isleworth Eyot we come to Twickenham Lock, the lowest of the checks to the flow of the Thames. It differs from all the others in being a 'half-tide lock' (i.e. the barrage can be raised or lowered as required), whereas all the 44 others have proper weirs, starting with Teddington Lock, $3\frac{1}{2}$ miles upstream.

Just after passing under the railway bridge (1848, J. Locke), we arrive at the waterfront of Richmond-upon-Thames. Looking ahead for 200 m we see a series of disconnected buildings, the first of them a fine stone mansion, Asgill House (1770, Robert Taylor). These are built on the site of the former Palace of Richmond which, before Hampton Court, was the principal royal palace upstream from London. In medieval times the place was called Shene (= Schöne). Here Henry I had a manor in 1125, and Edward III died in 1377. In 1394 the house was pulled down by Richard II in grief at the death of his wife who died of the plague in it; it was rebuilt by Henry IV, but destroyed by fire in 1499. On the site Henry VII, formerly Duke of Richmond, built a new palace covering nearly 10 acres and commanding the river front from what is now Old Palace Lane to Water Lane: the Habsburg Emperor Charles V visited him here. Henry VII and Elizabeth I both died here and Charles I held court. But then it was 'slighted' by the Parliamentarians, and subsequently declined in favour of Windsor and Hampton Court and, indeed,

Kew; and now all that remains of it is the old gateway, leading on to Richmond Green.

A short deviation is suggested for those wanting to see Richmond. This is to go up Old Palace Lane, right into and through Old Palace Yard, noticing Trumpeters' House and the Wardrobe; right again along the side of Richmond Green past Maid of Honour Row (1724), and right again into Friars' Lane to regain the river. Richmond Green should certainly not be missed: it is one of the most beautiful urban greens in England, with several eighteenth-century terraces, mansions, inns, and shops. There are other attractive areas and sites in Richmond, including the parish church of St Mary Magdalen (partly eighteenth-century tower and church), but they are to the other side of the busy and noisy shopping centre. In Georgian times, Richmond was certainly the most fashionable town near London. The great came here in the summer, often for short visits (indeed, the concept of the weekend away from town virtually originated at Richmond). Because of this, it attracted men of talent and genius. Dickens, Gainsborough, Reynolds, Sheridan and George Eliot all stayed here, and also Chateaubriand, that romantic exile, who has given us an admirable description of our Stage 2: '*Au-dessus de Londres, c'est l'Angleterre agricole et pastorale avec ses prairies, ses troupeaux, ses maisons de campagne, ses parcs, dont l'eau de la Tamise, refoulée par le flux, baigne deux fois le jour les arbustes et les gazons.*' Latterly, Leonard and Virginia Woolf established the Hogarth Press at Richmond, and published amongst other things T. S. Eliot's *The Waste Land*. Under the circumstances it was perhaps ungrateful of him to write in it that 'Richmond and Kew undid me'.

So ends Stage 2, the most urban of all the 16 Stages, but yet with a completely rural break at Brentford reach, so that at Kew one has the impression of leaving the big city unequivocally.

SPECIFICS

Over half Stage 3 is through parks and gardens, in which the going is easy and variously on paving, gravel, earth and grass. In between it leads through the town of Kingston by quiet terraced streets and riverside pavements. It passes a cluster of fine buildings at Petersham and culminates at Hampton Court Palace. Only just over a mile is near traffic.

ROUTE OUTBOUND

From Richmond Bridge to Hampton Court Bridge 6 miles (9·5 km)

(a) From Richmond Bridge to Kingston Bridge 4 miles (6·5 km)
At Richmond Bridge walk up the right bank of the Thames (left as you look upstream) past riverside boathouses. Where these end, by the Three Pigeons public house, take a path leading slightly away from the river through a public garden which leads close to, but does not cross, Petersham Road. At the end of the gardens, by a plaque denoting Devonshire Lodge, take a path ahead across Petersham Meadows and then between hedges and past Petersham Church to Petersham Road. Left along road for 150 m, then right through gate into Richmond Park. Through park, always keeping to path at lower edge of bank, for 1 mile to cross a park road just in front of Ham Gate; then for a further ¾ mile still along the lower edge of the hill, and close to the park wall, to the Kingston Gate. Into Park Road and immediately right into King's Road. King's Road passes to the right of the Richmond Park public house and later crosses Richmond Road. 200 m beyond, where King's Road veers left, continue straight ahead by King's Walk (with the power station immediately on the left) to reach the river. Then left along the riverside by Canbury Gardens, under an arch and then a railway bridge, on to Thameside and thence by Thames Street on to the upstream side of Kingston Bridge.

(b) From Kingston Bridge to Hampton Court Bridge 2 miles
(3·0 km)
Cross Kingston Bridge to the left bank of the Thames (right as you
look upstream) on the upstream side of the bridge. Continue ahead
until after passing a pedestrian crossing and traffic roundabout:
then enter left by Kingston Gate Lodge into Hampton Court Park
by a tarmac park road. After the fourth ramp (or third set of posts),
veer half right to enter the mile-long Kingston avenue which leads
through the park directly towards Hampton Court Palace. Enter the
palace gardens through a wrought-iron gate. Follow garden around
to the right, then left into an inner garden (the Wilderness), keeping
the palace to the left. From the Wilderness follow signs to the main
entrance. Then right to the Trophy Gates, and left on to Hampton
Court Bridge.

ROUTE INBOUND

From Hampton Court Bridge to Richmond Bridge 6 miles (9·5 km)

(a) From Hampton Court Bridge to Kingston Bridge 2 miles
(3·0 km)
At Hampton Court Bridge cross to the left bank of the Thames and
continue along the road for 50 m to turn right at the Trophy Gates
and up to the main entrance of Hampton Court Palace. Just before
the entrance turn left up a walled garden road, then turn right
through an inner garden (the Wilderness). On emerging onto the
open formal front garden proceed straight ahead to where a moat
borders the garden; then at the first opportunity leave the garden
through a wrought-iron gate into Hampton Court Park. This gate
leads straight into the mile-long Kingston avenue (not to be
confused with the canal avenue), at the end of which is seen the
tower of Kingston church. Follow the avenue to its extremity, then
pick up a tarmac park road which leads slightly left to Kingston
Gate Lodge. Right on to the pavement and on to Kingston Bridge.

(b) From Kingston Bridge to Richmond Bridge 4 miles (6·5 km)
Cross Kingston Bridge to the right bank of the Thames; then first

left at Thames Street and left again on to Thameside. Proceed downstream under railway bridge and then under an arch into the riverside Canbury Gardens. Immediately after passing the power station, turn right up King's Walk and then straight on up King's Road to its extremity at Park Road. Left at Park Road into Richmond Park. Keep along gravel path near to park wall on the left and at the lower edge of a hill for $\frac{3}{4}$ mile, then cross a tarmac park road in front of Ham Gate. Then straight ahead along a track for 1 mile always at the lower edge of the bank, and passing immediately to the right of Sudbrook Park golf course, and thence to the Petersham Gate. Left for 150 m along Petersham Road, then right into a lane passing by Petersham Church and thence between hedges and on across Petersham Meadows. Where this path enters gardens near to Petersham Road, continue through gardens ahead and down to the riverside as far as Richmond Bridge.

APPROACH BY CAR

Approach Richmond and Kingston are boroughs in Surrey and within Greater London, Richmond off the A316 leading to the M3 and Kingston near the A3 and on the A307. Hampton is in Middlesex and also within Greater London, on the A308. **Parking** For Richmond see Stage 2. Kingston: Cater's underground car park. Hampton Court: Palace car parking. **Taxis** Taxi ranks at Richmond (01-940 1549) and Kingston (01-546 1993).

APPROACH BY PUBLIC TRANSPORT

Trains London Transport and British Rail station at Richmond ($\frac{1}{2}$ mile from Richmond Bridge) and British Rail stations at Kingston ($\frac{1}{4}$ mile from Kingston Bridge) and Hampton (by Hampton Court Bridge). **Buses** Green Line at Richmond (the Quadrant), Kingston (bus station), and Hampton Court (Vrow Walk). **Boats** At Richmond, Kingston and Hampton Court.

PUBLIC TRANSPORT FROM END OF STAGE 3

To start of Stage 3 Green Line Bus from Hampton Court to
Richmond (hourly: journey time 21 minutes). Or Turks Boat (in
summer 5 times daily, journey time $\frac{1}{2}$ hour to Kingston and 1 hour
from Kingston to Richmond). **To start of Stage 2** Green Line buses
from Hampton Court to Hammersmith (two services, each hourly,
journey time 40 minutes). **To start of Stage 1** British Rail train
from Hampton to Waterloo (every $\frac{1}{2}$ hour, hourly on Sundays,
journey time 35 minutes). Or by Westminster Passenger Services
boat (three services daily in summer, May–September, journey time
4–5 hours).

ACCOMMODATION

Hotels For Richmond, see Stage 2; in Kingston, Hotel Antoinette,
28 Beaufort Road (01-546 1185); at Hampton, Greyhound Hotel,
Hampton Court Road, East Molesey (01-977 8121). **Guest houses
and small hotels** For Richmond, see Stage 2; in Kingston, Hotel
Olympos, 18 Lingfield Avenue (01-546 6408).

REFRESHMENT

Restaurants For Richmond, see Stage 2; Pembroke Lodge,
Richmond Park, and the Tiltyard, Hampton Court Palace (both
also have cafeteria); the Mitre, Hampton Court. **Pubs** Three
Pigeons, Richmond; Dysart Arms, Petersham; the Row-Barge,
Kingston; the Cardinal Wolsey, Hampton.

TIMES OF ADMISSION

Parks and Gardens Richmond Park: open all the time at the
Petersham Gate but at the Kingston Gate 07.00–dusk
March–November and 07.30–dusk December–February. Hampton
Court Park and Gardens: 07.00–dusk March–November and

07.30–dusk December–February. **Houses and Museums** Ham
House: daily except Mondays, 14.00–18.00 April–September, and
12.00–16.00 October–March; closed on winter bank holidays, Good
Friday and May Day. Hampton Court Palace: daily from 09.30
weekdays, and from 11.00 Sundays in summer and 14.00 in winter,
till 18.00 May–September, 17.00 March, April and October, and
16.00 November–February; closed winter bank holidays and Good
Friday.

FACILITIES

Tourist information Old Richmond Town Hall, Hill Street,
Richmond 01-892 0032).
Toilets Richmond, Kingston Gate of Richmond Park, Kingston
Bridge at Hampton Wick, Hampton Court.

DESCRIPTION

Which way, Amanda, shall we bend our course?
The choice perplexes. Wherefore should we choose?
All is the same with thee. Say, shall we wind
Along the streams? or walk the smiling mead?
Or court the forest glades? or wander wild
Among the waving harvests? or ascend,
While radiant summer opens all its pride,
Thy hill, delightful Shene?

James Thomson, 1700–48
from 'Summer'

Richmond Bridge is the lowest downstream of a series of elegant
eighteenth-century bridges that span the Thames. Although widened
and flattened in 1937, the original five-arch design of 1777 can still
be well seen. From it, our walk starts along Riverside with its series
of boathouses and pubs, and then through gardens in which a grotto
leads enticingly under the road to further gardens. Emerging from
the gardens into Petersham Meadows we get a good view of the
bend in the Thames and can see the roof of Ham House beyond
through fields, all made more picturesque by the herd of cattle that
often graze in them – the first sign of farming in our route out of
London. Up the hill to the left are houses on Richmond (formerly
Shene) hill. They enjoy a panoramic view, but we will do better to
postpone ours till we get into Richmond Park.

Petersham is a Georgian gem cut in half by a busy road. St Peter's
church is exquisite, and principally remarkable for its eighteenth-
century interior with box pews, two-decker pulpit and galleries. It is
an unusual sensation to attend a service there, enclosed in a box,
with disembodied heads participating from other parts of the

Montrose House, Petersham

church. Small is beautiful, and St Peter's happily escaped the
Victorian restorers and enlargers, whose energy was redirected in
building All Saints' down the road. St Peter's contains a
seventeenth-century memorial, and in the churchyard is buried
Captain George Vancouver, who surveyed the western coasts of
Canada 1791–4. Beyond, at the main road and to the right are four
fine houses. On the right of the road, Petersham House (late
seventeenth-century front) and Rutland Lodge (1666 and 1720); on
the left Reston Lodge (early nineteenth-century) and Montrose
House (early eighteenth-century). Their names betray their ducal
origins, of the time when Petersham was the most exclusive of all
summer resorts near London.

In later times a less blue-blooded but more brilliant man
frequented Petersham. Charles Dickens came here on several
occasions, in 1836 staying at the Dysart Arms and in 1839 renting
Elm Lodge. From 1838 he often stayed at the Star and Garter at
Richmond. When his best-selling serial *Pickwick Papers* had to be
wound up, it was to Richmond that he consigned his genial hero:
'Mr Pickwick settled, took lodgings at Richmond, where he has ever
since resided. He walks constantly on the terrace during the summer
months, with a youthful and jaunty air which has rendered him the
admiration of the numerous elderly ladies of single condition who
reside in the vicinity.'

Beyond them round to the left and then right at a lodge, a
deviation of 600 m would lead to Ham House, a great seventeenth-
century mansion owned in the latter part of that century by a vulgar
but powerful couple, the Countess of Dysart and her husband the
Duke of Lauderdale. It is rich in paintings, tapestries, furnishings,
plaster and woodwork. For those wanting to see Ham House it is
perfectly possible to continue along the right bank of the Thames all
the way up to Kingston Bridge. 'The choice perplexes . . .'; but I
have rejected this route in favour of one through Richmond Park,
because the park should not be missed, despite the urbanisation it
suffers as it enters Kingston.

Richmond Park is our first taste of real country since leaving
Whitehall. Although within Greater London, it is quite unlike the
central royal parks and much more like those of Windsor or
Blenheim. Like them, it originated as a medieval royal forest (a

forest was not a continuously wooded area, but an area which was
protected by special laws to safeguard the royal prerogative of
hunting the deer). But because it was so near London, this purpose
soon conflicted with commercial interests, and it was predictably
Charles I who provoked the issue by insisting, against advice, in
enclosing an area of the forest with a high wall to create a park
exclusively for hunting, and forcing out those who happened to live
within it. After the ensuing civil war and republican interlude,
Richmond Park came into its own, especially under George II.
When he was at White Lodge, Sir Robert Walpole, his First Lord of
the Treasury (and our first prime minister), was at Old Lodge. They
both thoroughly enjoyed their hunting, and there were certainly
thrills and spills as they pursued the stag. But I cannot help feeling
that by then the ceremonial aspects of venery had tamed it from
what it had been in medieval times. There were as many as 2,000
fallow deer in the park in 1669, so it cannot have been hard to kill a
stag!

The deer are still the main occupants of Richmond Park. They are
of two species. There are around 350 head of fallow deer (bucks,
does and fawns) and 250 of red deer (stags, hinds and calves).
Fawns are born in June and early July, calves in late May and June,
and the mother gives birth away from the rest of the herd, in
bracken or nettles. During the spring, the males' antlers fall off and
new ones form, covered in velvet. As the rutting season looms, the
males become restless and rub their antlers violently to remove the
velvet and prepare for battle. The season lasts for six weeks, with
roaring, fighting, mating and a lot of male chauvinism. In the
winter, the deer are fed, and special care is taken to see that the
calves and fawns get their share. In the park are also several
badgers, with some ten established setts: and foxes here, as
throughout the outer suburbs of London, are not uncommon.

A further fight for democracy was needed before Richmond Park
became accessible to the public, but this time it was not solved by
war, but by a circuit judge. The test case was induced by John
Lewis, who in 1758 contested the Royal Ranger's prohibition, as
enforced by one Martha Grey, a gatekeeper, of pedestrians going
through the park on ancient rights of way, and won the case. John
Lewis thus deserves our gratitude, a village Hampden upholding the

liberty of movement. Since then the park has become progressively accessible, though not at the expense of spoiling its natural state. It still comprises over 2,000 acres, and contains several thick plantations, fenced against the deer, and ponds in the centre. Riding is much in evidence, and near Ham Gate are stables for polo-ponies, which are frequently exercised in the park (especially between eight and ten o'clock in the morning) and are recognisable by their elegant gait and slow canter.

At the Petersham Gate, where we enter Richmond Park, a very worthwhile deviation is to go up the hill obliquely left and through a gate into the grounds of Pembroke Lodge. From Pembroke Lodge we can obtain our first panoramic view since leaving Whitehall. Looking down the hill we see the classic view of the Thames above Richmond, a view that has been so often painted – by Turner and Reynolds in particular. Looking further afield, we can also see Windsor Castle on a clear day, but contemplation of the intervening mass of urbanisation makes the longer view somewhat depressing. In the other direction, from just north of Pembroke Lodge, at Henry VIII's mound, a view eastwards to London can also be gained. At this high spot (56 m) a beacon would have been lit in times of emergency, and, according to Macaulay, at the time of the Spanish Armada

The sentinel on Whitehall Gate looked forth into the night
And saw o'erhanging Richmond Hill the streak of blood-red light.

Pembroke Lodge was leased to Earl Russell (Prime Minister 1846–51 and 1865–6), and later his grandson Bertrand Russell spent most of his childhood here, looked after by his formidable grandmother. The place had a strong formative influence on him, both from the Prime-Ministerial aura (it is said that the invasion of the Crimea in 1854 had been decided here at a Cabinet meeting at which several members were asleep) and high political tone; and also from the binding impression of the natural beauty on a lonely and sensitive child. 'I watched the sunset turn the earth red and the clouds golden: I listened to the wind, and exulted in the lightning.'

Reynolds: The Thames from Richmond Hill

Pembroke Lodge is now a restaurant and cafeteria; from it, the route can be regained by walking on through the garden, and thence obliquely down to the bottom of the hill.

At the bottom of the hill below Pembroke Lodge is Sudbrook Park, now a golf club. This was built (1726, James Gibbs) for the second Duke of Argyll, an all-powerful grandee of whom Dryden wrote

> Argyll in peace and war to none doth yield,
> Commands alike the senate and the field.

In *The Heart of Midlothian*, Walter Scott imagines a scene where the Duke of Argyle brings the heroine, Jeanie Deans, to plead for the life of her sister before Queen Caroline in Richmond Park. Jeanie had walked from Edinburgh. '"How far can you walk in a day?" "Five and twenty miles and a bittock." "And a what?" said the Queen, looking towards the Duke of Argyle. "And about five miles more," replied the Duke. "I thought I was a good walker," said the Queen, "but this shames me sadly." "May your Leddyship never hae sae weary a heart, that ye canna be sensible of the weariness of the limbs," said Jeanie.'

The two miles through Richmond Park are along the western edge and go through a long grove of oaks between Ham and Kingston Gates. Towards the end Thatched Lodge, built for Sir Robert Walpole, can be briefly seen at the top of the hill.

To get from Kingston Gate to the river we walk down King's Road, a residential street of Kingston. It consists of small villas of the 1870s and 80s, mostly well designed and with cheerful architectural features. Halfway down is the Richmond Park pub and the Roman Catholic church of St Agata (twentieth-century), and just after them the keep (1875), the guardhouse of a former military barracks. The overpowering presence of the Kingston power station at the riverside is softened by the trees which overlay our path along King's Walk and Canbury Gardens. And then we emerge on to the waterfront of Kingston-upon-Thames. This is surprisingly undeveloped, with empty spaces where one would expect buildings; a major development is planned, but the riverside walk will be protected and will also permit access under the bridge and so up the steps to it on the upstream side. The Thames here looks purposeful, with mooring-rafts on the near side and a timber yard on the far side. It was here at Kingston that Jerome K. Jerome embarked on his river expedition with his two companions, George and Harris, and the dog Montmorency, and wove from it his droll description of cheerful misadventure which created that Victorian bestseller *Three Men in a Boat*. In a fortnight they rowed up to Oxford, and then down river as far as Pangbourne, where they abandoned ship and fled by train to the raffish delights of Leicester Square.

This is a good point to admire Kingston Bridge (1828, Lapidge), and to note that the significance of Kingston in early history was that it was the lowest point on the Thames which was regularly (though not consistently) fordable. A bridge was built here as early as the thirteenth century, and for 500 years it was the nearest upstream from London Bridge. Kingston Bridge was of importance in the Wars of the Roses, when in 1452 Richard Plantagenet, Duke of York, having been refused entry into London by Henry VI, crossed by it into Surrey to effect his entry into the capital; also in the Civil War, when it was held by Parliament except for brief Royalist control in 1642 and 1648. As a footnote, Kingston Bridge was the last recorded place in England where a ducking-stool was used – in 1745 for a woman who kept the King's Head Inn, to punish her for 'scolding'! All this historical significance is hard to appreciate in a town which has shamefully destroyed nearly all its old buildings, but it can dimly be perceived by a short deviation of 300 m along Thames Street to Market Place. At the near end of this is All Saints' church (largely nineteenth-century but with thirteenth-century crossing piers and fourteenth-century nave arcades). At the far end, by the modern guildhall, is a block of grey sandstone which is believed to be a coronation stone on which six Saxon kings (Edward I, Athelstan, Edmund I, Edred, Edward II and Ethelred II) were crowned – presumably in an earlier church on or by the site of All Saints'.

After another noisy bridge-crossing we find haven in Hampton Court Park and very soon are steered towards Hampton Court along a truly magnificent mile-long avenue predominantly of limes. At the end of the vista, glimpses of the palace: in the rough grass around, fallow deer and sheep (the first we have encountered in the

whole Walk so far). This is the perfect way to approach a
destination, and eventually we arrive at an ornate iron gate through
which to enter the garden. Before leaving the Park, we should recall
that in it William III was thrown when his horse Sorrel tripped
(supposedly over a mole hill) in 1702, which caused his death a few
days later. Jacobites used to refer to the humble malefactor as 'the
little gentleman in black velvet'. But we can have reason to admire
William III because under him the new palace was built (1689–1702)
and the gardens were laid out in their present form; and these we
can best appreciate by walking up to the Great Fountain, and
thence to the Broad Walk in front of the palace, and looking back
to the semicircle of yews, the transverse avenue of limes, the
ornamental gates, and the triple vista into the home park with the
Charles II canal along the centre. Though it must be conceded that,
for sheer grandeur, even these avenues are eclipsed by the mile-long
avenue in Bushy Park, which may be glimpsed by walking to the
Lion Gates near the maze: it has two central lines of chestnuts
flanked by four lines of limes on each side. Limes are the dominant
trees around Hampton Court, and in 1978 those in the garden were
the subject of a correspondence in *The Times* (one of the last before
it closed for a year) on the age-old controversy of selective felling
versus wholesale replacement: selective felling won the day.

> Close by those meads forever crowned with flowers,
> Where Thames with pride surveys his rising towers,
> There stands a structure of majestic frame,
> Which from the neighbouring Hampton takes its name

– thus Alexander Pope, in *The Rape of the Lock*, introduces us to
the Palace, and thus we come up to its great east front, where 23
bays of windows on the first floor attest to the size of this English
emulation of Versailles by Christopher Wren, a frontage of which
the main feature is a stone centrepiece with corinthian columns and
decorative pediment.

Because we entered the grounds by an almost secret way, we have
to go around the palace to get to the entrance. Here is a surprise: a

Kingston Avenue, Hampton Court Park

Tudor building utterly different from the seventeenth-century 'Wrennaissance' we first saw. It is as if going from Versailles to Fontainebleau, or, in poetic analogy, from Pope to Shakespeare. For Hampton Court is in reality two palaces, each superb of its period. Wolsey's palace was the grandest in England, an architectural manifestation of his power which contributed to his downfall. But Henry VIII added further to it – the west-front wings and the Great Hall with its unparalleled hammer-beam roof – and made it his seat of power. This hall was later the scene of a crucial conference between the established church and the puritans in 1604, which failed to paper over the profound differences which became manifest during the Civil War, dramatically testified by the imprisonment and subsequent escape from Hampton Court by Charles I in 1647.

Hampton Court houses an important part of the royal picture collection, mainly Italian. These are mostly placed in the state rooms of the seventeenth-century palace, and the whole perambulation around the interior of Hampton Court is made all the better by the views from the windows on to the gardens. To these we eventually return, and, if we want, can see the Maze, the Great Vine, the Knot Garden and the Sunken Garden, before proceeding on towards Hampton Court Bridge. A backward look at the palace from the Trophy Gates gives a strange impression of towers and chimneys, a great complex red mass of 'majestic frame'.

Hampton Court is the upstream termination of the Thames boat passenger services which serve various points in Stages 1–3. A combination of walking and boating can add a dimension to an expedition: in his diary of 12 May 1662 Samuel Pepys records, 'Got to the barge and set out. We walked from Mortlake to Richmond, and so to boat again. And from Teddington to Hampton Court Mr Townsend and I walked again.' Thus it was that in the past the river was used in conjunction with walking.

SPECIFICS

This Stage is throughout along the bank of the Thames and virtually all away from traffic. It passes by five old riverside towns and between them is mostly encased in trees and bushes. It is mostly on gravel, though with sections on concrete and on earth.

ROUTE OUTBOUND

From Hampton Court Bridge to the Old Crown, Walton Lane, Weybridge 6 miles (10 km)

(a) From Hampton Court Bridge to Walton Bridge 4½ miles (7·5 km)
This stage proceeds uninterruptedly up the right bank of the Thames (left as you look upstream). From Hampton Court Bridge it starts along Riverbank to a war memorial, then right along a riverside drive past Molesey Lock. After Molesey boathouse it becomes a track which leads past Hurst Park and then past the brick walls and high banks of reservoirs. Soon after Sunbury Lock, at the Weir public house, an access road runs for some way parallel to the path, although separate from it. Later, after crossing the entrance to a marina by a girder bridge, the towpath leads under Walton Bridge.

(b) From Walton Bridge to the Old Crown, Walton Lane, Weybridge 1½ miles (2·5 km)
Continue up the right bank of the Thames (left as you look upstream) along a grass bank with a road parallel to the left. Where this road crosses the towpath by a bridge, continue straight ahead under the bridge, thereby leaving the mainstream of the Thames to enter the Desborough Cut. Over ½ mile on, under another bridge, the mainstream is regained; and the route then follows alongside the river. After Shepperton lock and weir can be seen on the further bank, the path joins a road, Walton Lane, and 200 m along it is the Old Crown public house.

ROUTE INBOUND

From the Old Crown, Walton Lane, Weybridge to Hampton Court Bridge 6 miles (10 km)

(a) From the Old Crown, Walton Lane, Weybridge to Walton Bridge $1\frac{1}{2}$ miles (2·5 km)
This stage proceeds uninterruptedly down the right bank of the Thames. From the Old Crown public house it starts down Walton Lane, but where the road leaves the riverside, the route takes to the towpath. After $\frac{1}{4}$ mile, the mainstream of the Thames turns away to the left, but the route goes straight ahead under a road bridge and alongside the Desborough Cut for over $\frac{1}{2}$ mile, to regain the mainstream under another bridge. Then along the river bank and under Walton Bridge.

(b) From Walton Bridge to Hampton Court Bridge $4\frac{1}{2}$ miles (7·5 km)
Continue down the right bank of the Thames along the towpath which leads by a girder bridge over the entrance to a marina. A mile further on, an access road runs for some way parallel to the path, although separate from it. After passing Sunbury lock, the towpath leads below the high banks and brick walls of reservoirs. After these it passes the Hurst Park housing estate and leads on to Molesey Lock. Then along Riverbank to cross Hampton Court Bridge.

APPROACH BY CAR

Approach Hampton is in Middlesex and within Greater London, on the A308. Walton and Weybridge are in Surrey, by the A3050 and not far from the London end of the M3. **Parking** Hampton Court: Palace car parking. Walton: Cowey Sale. Weybridge: in side streets off Walton Lane. **Taxis** Walton: Lawton Car Hire (tel. 40184) and taxi rank (tel. 21484). Weybridge: Gold Star Taxis (tel. 53538).

APPROACH BY PUBLIC TRANSPORT

Trains British Rail stations at Hampton (by Hampton Court

Bridge), Walton (1 mile from Walton Bridge), and Weybridge (1 mile from the Old Crown, Walton Lane, Weybridge). **Buses** Green Line at Hampton Court (Vrow Walk), Walton (Church Lane), and Weybridge (Ship).

PUBLIC TRANSPORT FROM END OF STAGE 4

To start of Stages 4, 3 and 2 Green Line bus from Weybridge to Hampton Court, Richmond, and Hammersmith respectively (hourly: journey time 22 minutes, 45 minutes, and 1 hour, respectively).
To start of Stage 1 Train from Weybridge to Waterloo (half-hourly: journey time 30 minutes).

ACCOMMODATION

Hotels For Hampton Court, see Stage 3; East Molesey, Thames Hotel (01-979 6249); Weybridge, Ship Hotel (tel. 48364) and Oatlands Park Hotel (tel. 47242). **Camping** Camping Club of Great Britain site: Fieldcommon Lane, Hersham, 2 miles from Walton Bridge (Walton 20392) – open April–September.

REFRESHMENT

Restaurant The Mitre, Hampton Court. **Pubs** The Weir, Sunbury Lock; the Swan, Walton; the Old Crown, Weybridge.

TIMES OF ADMISSION

Houses and Museums Hampton Court Palace: see Stage 3.

FACILITIES

Tourist information Information Centre, Elmbridge Borough Council, Town Hall, Walton (tel. 25141).
Toilets Walton Bridge; upstream end of Desborough Cut.

DESCRIPTION

Along the shore of silver streaming Thames;
Whose rutty bank, the which his river hems,
Was painted all with variable flowers,
And all the meads adorned with dainty gems
Fit to deck maidens' bowers,
And crown their paramours
Against the bridal day, which is not long:
Sweet Thames! run softly, till I end my song.

Edmund Spenser, 1552(?)–99
from 'Prothalamion'

A short way downstream of Hampton Court Bridge (1933,
Lutyens), the Thames receives the tributary of the river Mole.
Between Box Hill and Leatherhead this small river runs through
fissures or 'swallows' in the chalk; and pastoral poets made great
play of this – as Milton's 'the sullen Mole, that runneth underneath'.
This confluence is the reason why the second Thames lock and weir
is to be found at Molesey, just upstream. From the right bank we
can see the weir, which was painted by Sisley in a famous blue and
white picture. But we have a better opportunity to inspect the lock,
which we go right past, as also Sunbury lock further up, finishing
with a glimpse of Shepperton lock. These lower Thames locks were
constructed in the early nineteenth century and before them the
Thames was tidal as far up as Staines. This was an important factor
for river transport, and greatly helped the ease of movement
between London and all the houses and palaces we have seen in
Stages 2–3. But water control even in these lower reaches became
inevitable with the advent of steam. The means of control were weirs
and pound locks.

The principle of the pound lock is beautifully simple, and it is
surprising that it only became properly developed in the late

fifteenth century. The whole object is to arrange for the minimum amount of water to escape to a lower level whilst raising boats upstream to a higher level. This control was first achieved on Chinese and Dutch canals in the fourteenth century by the use of stop-log gates which at certain points were close enough together to achieve this effect, and in Holland portcullis gates were also used. But in northern Italy in the fifteenth century, especially in the canals around Milan, the technique was improved; and it was Leonardo da Vinci who first sketched out the design of mitre gates with vertical sluices, for the San Marco canal lock on the Naviglio Interno at Milan in 1495. The principle requires a chamber with vertical walls and at each end a pair of solid wooden gates which close obliquely on to sills at the bottom of the water: the downstream sill is lower than the upstream sill, and both can withstand enormous pressure. Water is then let in or out of the lock by means of the sluice gates. Obviously, the size of the lock will be as small as is consonant with the type of boat and the amount of traffic. For these reasons, Thames locks are small compared to their Continental counterparts, because the Thames itself is so much smaller than the main European rivers and canals.

The second feature of the Thames to note in this Stage is the towpath along which we walk. Towing boats upstream beyond the tidal reaches was far easier than the time-honoured alternatives of rowing, poling or sailing. Men as well as horses towed the boats, and large barges needed gangs of men or teams of horses. The standard barge of the nineteenth century was known as the Western Barge, and it had a maximum length of 128 ft, a beam of 18 ft, a draught of 4 inches and a capacity of 200 tons.

After Molesey we pass a well-designed new housing estate which is on part of a former open space called Hurst Park. The housing is sensibly set back from the river, and is only disfigured by one tower block. In the eighteenth century Moulsey Hurst (as it was called) was a great place for prize-fights, those bloody, bare-fisted boxing bouts which achieved an enormous following in all classes. It was also an early centre for less violent sports. In 1723 the Gentlemen of London played the Gentlemen of Surrey at cricket, and both teams were afterwards entertained by the Prince of Wales at Hampton Court: and the East Molesey Cricket Club dates from a match here

in 1730. And in 1758 we hear of David Garrick playing golf on Moulsey Hurst. Later, a racecourse was built, but now sport has given way to housing on Hurst Park.

On the opposite bank is Hampton. St Mary's church (1831) is flanked by some nice houses and cottages. Just downstream from it is Hampton House, bought by David Garrick and altered for him (by Robert Adam in 1755). We cannot see it well because of an intervening road, but we get a good view of the octagonal Shakespeare temple, built to house a statue of the bard. Garrick was a great actor who revolutionised the English stage: he 'banished ranting, bombast and grimace and restored nature, ease, simplicity and genuine humour'. He had a great gift for friendship and when he retired here in financial security, a flow of fashionable and cultivated people came to visit him. There were *fêtes-champêtres* and conversaziones, and the *Gentleman's Magazine* of 1774 records that 'the Temple of Shakespeare, and the gardens, were illuminated with 6,000 lamps and a Forge of Vulcan made a splendid appearance'.

Our way upstream now passes between reservoirs on either bank. The Molesey Reservoir on our side is bordered by a brown brick wall with intervening pilasters which makes for a secluded stretch of towpath which is not unpleasing. Although it is termed a towpath, towing here would in fact be impossible because of the bushes between the path and the river: they include particularly good blackberries, and a walker here in September may freely sample several species. Along this stretch we also encounter a group of plain cubes of concrete, which are examples of the tank barriers placed at tactical points all over southern England in 1940 when German invasion seemed imminent. Various eyots also help to protect us from the road and built-up area on the further bank, though not so much as to prevent a charming view of old Sunbury, which has the appearance of a small seaport.

After the Sunbury lock cut the further bank is unobstructed from our view, but by then it fortunately has no road and supports merely a succession of waterfront bungalows which appear very vulnerable to flooding. On our side, just after Sunbury lock is the Weir public house, a good place for a halt. The only disadvantage of

Zoffany: Mr and Mrs Garrick by the Shakespeare Temple at Hampton

the Weir to us is that its approach road runs parallel to our path for half a mile and brings desultory motorists to cruise and park along it. The scene is enlivened by the new Elmbridge Leisure Centre, and soon afterwards we come to Walton-on-Thames, and past several riverside houses of character and old walls and gardens.

St Mary's Walton is off course by a quarter of a mile but is worth a detour, made by turning away from the river just by the Swan public house, and then left along the road. The church (fourteenth-century with Norman remains and nave roof of 1630) is of flint and with a robust tower; but the main attraction is the spectacular monument to Richard Boyle, Viscount Shannon, by Roubiliac (1755), a great military montage with gun, gun-carriage, flag, tent, tree, drum, apotheosis of languid field-marshal, and ritual mourning by dutiful daughter. Walton bridge, which we now approach, is different from the bridge painted by Turner from the same aspect. And Turner's bridge in its turn was different from that which had earlier been painted by Canaletto, an unusually rustic scene for the cosmopolitan Venetian to choose. Canaletto's bridge was a wooden structure which was built in a complete semicircle; and it was said that any member of it could be extracted without disturbing any of the other members.

But Walton is not of importance only for these artistic and engineering achievements. In earlier history, its main significance was that it was a ford. And 200 m upstream from the bridges was a point where several wooden stakes – known as the Cowey stakes – sunk in the mud, excited the curiosity of early historians. It has been plausibly suggested that these stakes were associated with the advance by the Romans led by Julius Caesar across the Thames in AD 54 to defeat the British leader Cassivellaunus. In Caesar's own words, the river could be crossed at only one point on foot, and that with difficulty ('*quod flumen uno omnino loco pedibus, atque hac aegre, transiri potest*'); and when they did so, they encountered the British defences on the further bank, which was fortified with a fringe of sharp projecting stakes ('*ripa autem erat acutis sudibus praefixis munita*'). Whether this crossing and a subsequent Roman causeway occurred here or at Brentwood or Kingston cannot be

Canaletto: Old Walton Bridge

firmly established, but the Cowey – or causeway – stakes at Walton can at any rate stake their claim!

We are on surer ground in noting that when the eighteenth-century bridge was constructed, several funerary barrows, indicating prehistoric settlement, were razed; and also that (as explained in my notes on place-names) Walton was certainly a place inhabited by the British in the early centuries of our era.

The long-distance nature of the Walk requires the elimination of unnecessary diversions, and so it leads along the Desborough cut when the river makes a couple of sharp loops near Shepperton. But those who do not mind an extra $\frac{3}{4}$ mile would do well to go by the river and there encounter an unspoilt corner, and see Shepperton church and square picturesquely situated on the far bank. To the south of the Desborough cut lay Oatlands, a Tudor palace of which nothing now remains: the cedars which were planted there by Prince Henry, son of Charles I, were possibly the first ever to be planted in England. The cut and the river soon reunite and come to a wide pool of water below Shepperton lock – the southernmost point of the Thames and of our Walk. This is where the river Wey and the Wey navigation canal together join the Thames. The weir at Shepperton is often used by canoeists, testing their skill in the restricted turbulence.

Anyone walking Stage 4 will be unlucky if he does not see swans. These beautiful birds have enjoyed a special form of royal protection – indeed, ever since they were introduced into England, supposedly from Cyprus at the time of the Crusades. The Crown appoints a Swan Keeper to look after the swan population of around 500 between Blackfriars, in London, and Henley. Every summer he supervises the 'Swan Upping', in which cygnets' beaks are marked.

Stage 4 is also a good place to note the Thames Conservancy's admirable experiment in trying to reintroduce salmon, now that pollution has been so much reduced. This rehabilitation project has involved the introduction of some 50,000 marked salmon parr in tributaries of the Thames in 1979. In 1980, these will have grown to smolts 6–7 inches long, which will swim out to sea. Four years later, in 1984, it is hoped that the grown salmon (8–10 lbs or more) will come back up the Thames past Teddington weir and Molesey weir (at which a run will be built for them); and, if the experiment is successful, to upper reaches in subsequent years.

In terms of heritage values, Stage 4 is relatively undistinguished. But it provides a straight and secluded route through a heavily populated area 'along the shore of silver-streaming Thames'.

SPECIFICS

The first half of Stage 5 negotiates the waters of the Wey and the
muddy fields of Chertsey Mead into the old centre of Chertsey.
The second half leads along a well-maintained grass path through
the Water Park to the quiet village of Thorpe, and thence by less
well-maintained paths with muddy patches up to the edge of
Windsor Great Park. Somewhat over 2 miles is on streets, all quiet
ones.

ROUTE OUTBOUND

**From the Old Crown, Walton Lane, Weybridge, to the corner of the
A30 and Wick Road, Englefield Green** 8 miles (13 km)

*(a) From the Old Crown, Walton Lane, Weybridge to Abbey Green,
Chertsey* $3\frac{1}{2}$ miles (5·5 km)
At Walton Lane find the Old Crown public house: beside it, turn
into Church Walk. Follow on, across a road, and continue for
100 m to where another concrete path leads to the right, in front of
cottages. Take this path and cross footbridge over the Wey, to
arrive at a road with factory gates on the left marked 'private'. To
the right of these gates take a narrow footpath which leads over a
steep footbridge over the Wey Navigation Canal. Turn left up the
left-bank towpath of this canal for over half a mile until a high brick
bridge crossing the canal can be seen ahead. Find a convenient place
to get off the towpath across an intervening ditch to an unpaved
road. Retrace direction rightwards along this lane till, where it veers
right, a signposted footpath leads left. Follow this over a decrepit
stile and then across a field towards a caravan site. Then go along
the edge of the caravan site to the right, keeping close to it when it
turns, to reach an unpaved farm road. Turn right along this road
and cross the Bourne by a concrete bridge. Then on, keeping the
Bourne stream close to the left for well over $\frac{1}{4}$ mile. Then, at a point
between the first and second pylons after the pylon by the concrete

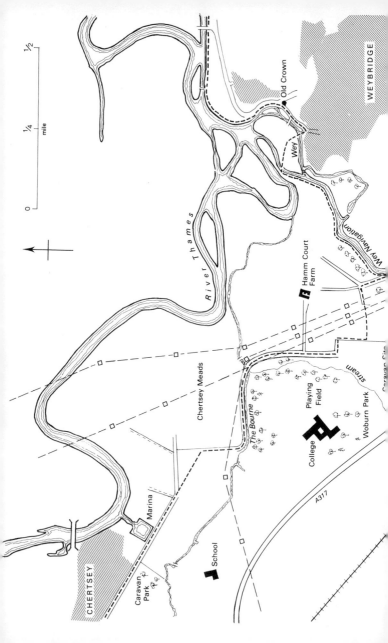

CHERTSEY

WEYBRIDGE

Old Crown

Wey

Wey Navigation

Hamm Court Farm

Chertsey Meads

River Thames

Caravan Park

Marina

School

The Bourne

College

Playing Field

Woburn Park

Caravan Site

Woburn Park stream

A317

0   ¼   ½
mile

bridge, leave the Bourne and turn right along a track beside a fence into the middle of Chertsey Mead. At a point where there is a stile in the fence, turn left on to a track which joins a tarmac road (Mead Lane). Passing a marina on the right, continue to the end of Mead Lane. Across Weir Road into Stepgates. At end, turn right on to a road which shortly becomes Pound Road. At a junction of four streets, cross London Street-Abbey Road to enter Bridge Road. 50 m on, just past the Vine public house, turn left on to a signposted bridleway, which becomes Willow Lane and leads to Abbey Green.

(b) From Abbey Green, Chertsey to the corner of the A30 and Wick Road, near Englefield Green 4½ *miles* (7·5 km)

When we arrive at Abbey Green from Willow Lane, the first exit (in a clockwise direction) is the pedestrian Church Approach. The next (at this end unmarked) is Colonel's Lane, which we take to lead us to Windsor Street. Right at Windsor Street, then straight ahead along Staines Lane. At end, follow a path which leads up the bank of a main road. Then turn right to cross the road bridge over the M3 motorway. Then follow a footpath sign to descend the bank on the far side of the motorway, and to pass under the road bridge. Proceed along a footpath between wire fences through Thorpe Water Park. After this, straight ahead across a stile along a path between hedges to a stone stile; and so past Church Approach, Thorpe, ahead along a road (Coldharbour Lane). Then at a fork, by the Red Lion public house, turn right on to the B388 road. A quarter of a mile on, immediately after a shop, turn left on to a path signposted to Prune Hill. At end, turn half right for 50 m along a lane (Muckhatch Lane), and then across a road and by a farm access bridge over the M25. Off the bridge down and slightly right, then ahead through a belt of wood and along the edge of two fields. Straight across a road on to a signposted path to a small wooden footbridge: then across a field to a point immediately to the left of two cottages near together. On to a road signposted for Englefield Green. Just before a railway crossing, turn left on to a path signposted for Callow Hill; after 50 m this path crosses the railway. Follow along outside the lower edge of a wood: where the wood resumes after a small gap, take the second of two stiles with paths leading up into the wood. The path from the second stile leads leftwards: after going up and then down, it soon has a field on the left. Where the field ends, take a path to the right across a boggy patch, and then uphill with a field on the right. At a road (Callow Hill) turn left: then, after 100 m, right on to a signposted footpath leading up an avenue and then across a field to reach the A30 road. Cross the A30 and walk 200 m right to the corner of Wick Road.

ROUTE INBOUND

From the corner of the A30 and Wick Road, Englefield Green, to the Old Crown, Walton Lane, Weybridge 8 miles (13 km)

(a) From the corner of the A30 and Wick Road, Englefield Green, to Abbey Green, Chertsey $4\frac{1}{2}$ miles (7·5 km)

At the top of Wick Road turn right to walk 200 m along the footpath beside the A30. Then cross the A30 to find a path across a field, signposted for Bakenham Lane. This path passes to the right of a pond and continues across a field and into an avenue. At a road (Callow Hill) turn left for 100 m, then right at a path signposted for Prune Hill. The path leads downhill and then across a marshy patch. At end, where it meets another path just before a field, turn left. The path leads up and then down through a wood and to a stile. Across the stile, then left along the outside lower edge of a wood and thence across a railway line; then left to a road. Turn right along this road for 200 m to a point where it bears left. Here, to the right of a cottage and just by the entrance to a farm, a signposted path leads through a gate and into a field. Walk to the far end of the field to a small wooden footbridge over a marshy patch. Beyond this the path leads on, to arrive at a road. Cross the road and proceed along the edge of two fields and through a belt of trees, and then cross the M25 by a farm access bridge, then across a road into Muckhatch Lane: after 50 m, turn left on to a footpath leading initially alongside a wall and then past gardens, to the B388 road. Turn right on this road into Thorpe. At the Red Lion public house turn left into Coldharbour Lane. At Church Approach, half right over a stone stile to path signposted for Chertsey. After a short section between hedges this footpath leads for 1 mile between wire fences

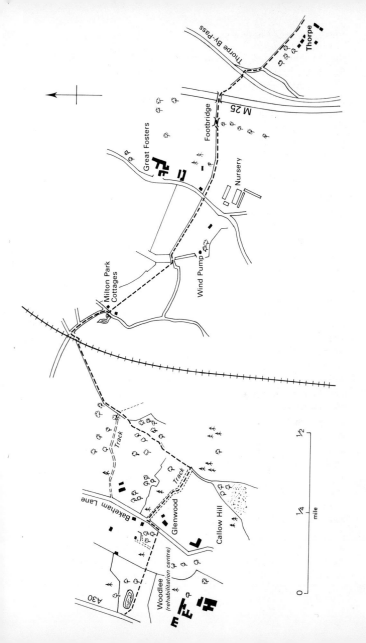

through the Thorpe Water Park. Go under a road bridge, then
follow the path leading up the bank to the road. Turn left to cross
over the M3 motorway. Then down the bank on the further side at a
footpath sign. This path leads into Staines Lane. Along Staines
Lane, continuing briefly in Windsor Street, before turning left into
Colonel's Lane, and thence to Abbey Green.

*(b) From Abbey Green, Chertsey, to the Old Crown, Walton Lane,
Weybridge* 3½ miles (5·5 km)
From Abbey Green take a pedestrian passage marked Willow Walk,
which is also a bridleway. This emerges at Bridge Road by the Vine
public house. Turn right into Bridge Road, and 50 m later cross
London Street-Abbey Road into Pound Road. First left into
Stepgates. Cross Weir Road into Mead Lane. Soon after passing a
marina on the left, where the road veers left, continue straight ahead
by a path in a field. At a fence, turn right along a track beside the
fence, to the edge of the mead, and then follow it around to the left,
along the edge of the Bourne stream. The track crosses the Bourne
by a concrete bridge and continues parallel to a line of pylons. Just
before a caravan site, turn left into a field and follow the outside of
the caravan site around to the right. After 100 m, having crossed a
fence, strike left at a footpath sign across a field to a stile and on
into a second field to a lane. Turn right along this lane to a point
where it is convenient to cross an intervening ditch on the left to
gain the towpath of the Wey Navigation Canal. Having gained the
canal towpath, turn left and follow the canal downstream to a lock.
Cross the canal by a steep bridge, and then along a path. Where this
joins a factory access road, cross the road to traverse the Wey by an
iron footbridge. After passing cottages, turn left along a passageway
which crosses one road and leads to the Old Crown public house in
Walton Lane.

APPROACH BY CAR

Approach Weybridge, Chertsey and Englefield Green are all in
Surrey, not far from the London end of the M3: Weybridge on the
A317, Chertsey on the A320 and Englefield Green on the A30.

Parking In Weybridge, park in side-streets off Walton Lane near the Old Crown public house. In Chertsey, car park in Heriot Road. At Englefield Green, use the Windsor Great Park car park in Wick Road. **Taxis** Weybridge: Gold Star taxis (tel. 53538). Chertsey: taxi rank (tel. 62206). Egham: Union Jack Hire (tel. 4026) and taxi rank (tel. 3195).

APPROACH BY PUBLIC TRANSPORT

Trains British Rail stations at Weybridge (1 mile from the Old Crown, Walton Lane), Chertsey ($\frac{1}{2}$ mile from St Peter's, Chertsey), and Egham ($\frac{3}{4}$ mile from Prune Hill). **Buses** Green Line at Weybridge (Ship) and Englefield Green (Holly Tree $\frac{1}{2}$ mile from corner of A30 and Wick Road).

PUBLIC TRANSPORT FROM END OF STAGE 5

To start of Stage 5 To Egham station walking, or by Green Line from Englefield Green (half-hourly: journey time 5 minutes), and then train from Egham to Weybridge (half-hourly, hourly on Sundays: journey time 18 minutes).
To start of Stage 4 Green Line from Englefield Green to Hampton Court (half-hourly: journey time 40 minutes). **To start of Stage 3** Green Line or Alder Valley from Englefield Green to Staines station (half-hourly: journey time 12 minutes), and then train from Staines to Richmond (half-hourly: journey time 17 minutes). **To start of Stage 2** Inconvenient: same as for start of Stage 3; then at Richmond take Richmond line train to Hammersmith (every 20 minutes with journey time of 10 minutes).

ACCOMMODATION

Hotels For Weybridge, see Stage 4. Egham: Great Fosters (tel. 3822). **Guest houses and small hotels** Chertsey: Bridge Hotel (tel. 63175). **Group accommodation** Royal Holloway College (Egham 34455). **Camping** Camping Club of Great Britain site, Bridge Road, Chertsey (tel. 62405) – open all year.

REFRESHMENT

Restaurants The Wheatsheaf, Virginia Water. The Bailiwick, Wick Road, Englefield Green. **Snacks** At Weybridge and Chertsey.
Pubs The Old Crown, Walton Lane, Weybridge; the Vine, Bridge Road, Chertsey; the Red Lion, Thorpe.

TIMES OF ADMISSION

Parks and gardens Thorpe Water Park: 10.00–18.00 daily.

FACILITIES

Telephones Cheeseman's Gate, Wick Road.

DESCRIPTION

Nor are his blessings to his banks confined,
But free and common as the sea or wind,
When he, to boast or to disperse his stores,
Full of the tribute of his grateful shores,
Visits the world, and in his flying towers
Brings home to us, and makes both Indies ours;
Finds wealth where 'tis, bestows it where it wants,
Cities in deserts, woods in cities, plants.

John Denham, 1615–69
from 'Cooper's Hill'

Just below Shepperton lock, near the end of Stage 4, the Thames
towpath crosses to the further bank, but in the absence of bridge,
ferry or lock-crossing, we cannot follow it. Even if we could, it
would provide a rather unsatisfactory route to Chertsey Abbey
Green – the end of the first half of this Stage.

So instead our Stage starts past some charming cottages in
Thames-side Weybridge, which is older and of more character than
the main centre of the town: and from them we come to the Wey
Navigation Canal, now owned by The National Trust. This
waterway formerly connected with the Arun canal and thus with the
south coast, forming an important strategic link before the railway
age. This short stretch is flanked by a wood: and on the canal we
may with luck see a long-boat, the traditional canal wooden barge;
some of them are brightly painted with strange designs and rural
scenes.

Chertsey Mead and the adjoining fields south of the Bourne
stream would be a perfectly pleasant open space of large fields
fringed with trees, were it not for the dominating and forbidding

Wey Navigation Canal lock

triple line of high-tension-wire pylons, which stride across it like giants while we petty men walk under their huge legs and peep about. Besides, the route from the canal bank across the first part of the Mead is very boggy and, if we scrupulously obeyed the footpath sign, we should walk right into what in winter is a small pond! This area (together with the fields before Prune Hill later in this Stage) may be considered as the 'Slough of Despond' for Thames Valley Heritage Walkers, but will not test them as severely as Christian in Bunyan's *Pilgrim's Progress*: 'Now, I saw in my dream, that just as they had ended this talk they drew near to a very miry slough, that was in the midst of the plain; and they, being heedless, did both fall suddenly into the bog. The name of the Slough was Despond. Here, therefore, they wallowed for a time, being grievously bedaubed with dirt; and Christian, because of the burden on his back, began to sink in the mire.' After this we pass the commonplace residences of Mead Lane and Stepgates, with names such as 'Simla', 'Penshurst', 'For-T-For' and, best of all, 'Dunromin'.

Chertsey is a town with an important medieval history which has subsequently been unfortunate, first through the destruction of its abbey and latterly by the unsightly development of the surrounding locality. Chertsey Abbey was originally a Benedictine foundation of the seventh century, and in those Saxon times it rated with Westminster and Abingdon as one of the three leading religious institutions in the whole of the Thames valley, the early purveyors of civilisation in a land of primitive tribesmen. The first great challenge to this early Christian culture was from the invasions of the pagan Danes in the ninth century, and Chertsey was then utterly destroyed. But its recolonisation and reconstruction under Norman rule was more splendid than before, and it was progressively enriched by gifts of lands, including nearly all our route in Stage 5: 'Come now towards Chertsey with your holy load,' writes Shakespeare on the temporary interment of Henry VI at the abbey.

The second challenge came from the Reformation, by the enforced dissolution of the monasteries. With this neither Chertsey nor any others (except for some cathedral foundations) could compete. But Chertsey had the added indignity of being systematically dismantled, so that most of its best stones could be floated down river to be used in the construction of Hampton

Court. So now there is virtually nothing left of Chertsey Abbey, though we do pass a bricked-up stone arch on the wall of Colonel's Lane, and some stones placed in the wall of Willow Walk look strongly as though they came from a grander edifice. Encaustic tiles, for which the abbey was famous, are preserved at the British and Victoria and Albert museums in London.

Subsequently Chertsey was mainly known as a staging-point on the main road towards Basingstoke and the south-west. William Cobbett passed through it on one of his rural rides and found 'everything exceedingly dull'; and our contemporary architectural gazetteer, Nikolaus Pevsner, goes so far as to describe St Peter's nave (1808) as a 'repellent piece of Gothick': but Chertsey has several houses of character, especially in London Street. Our route into the town is undistinguished, but when we get to the bridleway to Abbey Green and Colonel's Lane we pass gardens, walls and the backs of houses which give a pleasurable impression.

The church's chancel is fourteenth-century and its tower is of medieval construction: it has the curious distinction of being the last parish church in England to ring the curfew (till 1939), a tradition which is said to have inspired Rose H. Thorpe to write her poem 'Curfew shall not ring tonight'. Another poetic association is that Abraham Cowley, that prolific seventeenth-century Poet Laureate, lived in retirement at Chertsey. A curious episode in Dickens' *Oliver Twist* occurs when Bill Sikes takes Oliver down there from London to rob a house. They start their journey by walking from Whitechapel to Kensington, then hitch a lift to Isleworth; then walk from Isleworth to Hampton, and after another lift in a cart, walk by night from Shepperton to Chertsey. I calculate that the unfortunate Oliver had to cover 14 miles on foot to the scene of the crime!

After negotiating the crossing of the M3, we are out of Chertsey and into an area where the wholesale excavation of gravel has created a series of artificial lakes. These have recently been landscaped, stocked with wildfowl, and generally smartened to create the Thorpe Water Park, where various aquatic activities take place in a suitable setting. Fortunately for us a footpath, known as the Monk's Way, leads right through the middle of the area, and so we obtain a transient enjoyment without having to pay the entry fee into the park.

To our left can be seen St Anne's Hill, on which traces of a bank and ditch are thought to be the remains of an Iron Age enclosure. More recently, St Anne's Hill became a fashionable area of residence, and Charles James Fox lived in a house on it. He acquired it from the Crown Estates and there is a strong suspicion that, as leader of the Opposition in the House of Commons at the time, he accepted it as a gift for not pressing for a debate on a government scandal actually involving the Crown Estates!

Thorpe is our first distinct village since leaving London, and not until Cookham in Stage 8 do we come to a scene comparable to the one we get in Church Approach and Coldharbour Lane. Opposite Church Approach is an early eighteenth-century house (Renalds) which has preserved its 'heavy glazing' (or thick window frames); and behind the brick walls of Coldharbour Lane are two large eighteenth-century houses – Spelthorne St Mary on the left and Thorpe House on the right. St Mary's Church has a seventeenth-century brick tower, and an interior which includes a twelfth-century chancel arch and beyond, within the chancel, fourteenth-century items such as two unusual sedilia (seats for priests) and windows in the north side. There are two sixteenth-century brasses set in the chancel floor, one to John Bonde (who had seven sons and seven daughters) and the other to William Denham (five sons and ten daughters). Although most of these presumably perished in infancy, the Denhams were still living at Thorpe in the eighteenth century and included one of William's grandsons, John Denham, who contemplated the Thames from Cooper's Hill nearby. (In his reference to the 'flying towers', the poet possibly had a premonition of the aircraft taking off and landing at Heathrow in continuous succession; but of the disappearance of the British Empire, he evidently had none.)

On a more practical plane, it should be noted that the Red Lion at Thorpe is the last pub on our route for 6 miles (to Bishopsgate), and the village general store (further on, where the footpath starts) the last for 9 miles.

A flat section, bisected by a motorway, brings us to a point from which we can see the roofs and towers of Great Fosters. This is one

Thorpe Church Approach

of the best sixteenth-century country houses in Surrey, and it is well worth deviating for 200 m up the road to take a look at it, and indeed to wander around the gardens, which can be entered by permission from the management. The Elizabethan front is imposing, but the best impression is from the formal garden where the square staircase towers add an unusual touch to the complicated ensemble. Great Fosters was converted into a hotel in the 1920s, and it soon became a fashionable place for private dinners and parties, patronised by the Prince of Wales. It still fulfils the role, and a tasteful extension has been added to cater for business conferences. Great Fosters provides a luxurious, though expensive, overnight resting-place for through-walkers. The impression is more that of a country house than a hotel, and those who have walked many miles to get there can feel that they have indeed earned their luxury, as they lay into a good dinner in the panelled dining room, or sit in the front hall with the Jacobean fireplace, or mount by the oak well staircase to their bedrooms. Incidentally, the name Great Fosters derives from the fact that Windsor forest formerly extended into this area, and the house was built at a forester's lodge. Great Fosters has been occupied by a number of aristocratic families, including those of Thynne (Marquesses of Bath) and Percy (Dukes of Northumberland).

Turning our eyes away from Great Fosters we can discern a line of small hills ahead. On top of one of the hills is a truly remarkable cluster of turrets, towers, gables, chimneys and pediments. This is the Royal Holloway College, a women's college (now mixed) built by W. H. Crossland in 1887 to the orders of Thomas Holloway. Crossland was given a free hand in his design, and he has succeeded in producing a startling imitation of the French sixteenth-century style, and in particular of Chambord. One does not grudge Holloway College its commanding position, as one does the architecturally dull Star and Garter Home on Richmond Hill. Incidentally, it contains a picture gallery including paintings by Gainsborough, Moreland, Constable, Turner, Landseer, Millet and Frith, which can be seen by appointment. The rich benefactor also financed the Holloway Sanatorium whose large nineteenth-century

The chimneys of Great Fosters

Continental-Gothic tower can be seen lower down and to our left.

To reach the higher ground ahead we have to traverse some low-lying fields. At one point a wooden footbridge helps us over a pond, but in wet weather will not protect us from surrounding mud. There is no alternative to this short of diverting through Egham, which is not recommended. But the second, and less boggy, section of pasturage which comes after the railway crossing, could be avoided by continuing up the road to Prune Hill that crosses the railway and, when it reaches the A30, turning left and along the A30 for over $\frac{1}{4}$ mile to the end of Stage 5. From the higher ground we can get a good view looking back – a view described by John Aubrey in his 'Brief Life' of John Denham: '. . . Prune-well-hill (formerly part of Sir John's possessions) where was a fine tuft of trees, a clear spring, and a pleasant prospect to the east, over the level of Middlesex and Surrey. Sir John took great delight in this place . . .'

So ends Stage 5, a stage which with Stage 4 leads us from the oases of Richmond and Hampton Court out through the mass of modern megalopolis towards carefully conserved areas of countryside in Berkshire and Buckinghamshire. It has its own character, not so much of national heritage as of local attributes; and is full of interest and, I hope, enjoyment.

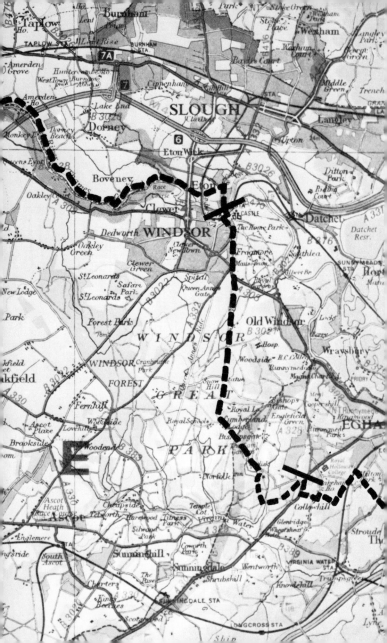

SPECIFICS

This Stage is entirely through Windsor Great Park, leading to
Windor castle and town, which comprise the last half-mile. In the
Park the walks and rides are all very well kept up, and mud should
present no problem. In the middle of the park we come to the best
panorama of the entire Walk.

ROUTE OUTBOUND

**From the corner of the A30 and Wick Road, Englefield Green, to
Windsor Bridge** 6½ miles (10·5 km)

At the corner of the A30 and Wick Road enter Windsor Great Park
by a small gate. Take path leading away from both roads into the
wood, at a fork keeping close to plantation palings and going
downhill. At the end of a straight ride turn left across a watercourse,
and then right alongside it to Virginia Water. Cross by pathway
between upper and lower water to Totem Pole. At Totem Pole, and
later at park crossroads, follow signs for Savill Garden, passing by
Obelisk Pond. At the Obelisk, take the ride which leads downhill
and across a stone bridge, with Savill Garden on the right, and
along the edge of Smith's Lawn to Cumberland Gate. Go through
the gate and turn half left through trees on to a grass track. Pass to
the right of Cumberland Lodge and its tennis court, and on ahead
to the palings of Royal Lodge. Keep close to the left of these
palings, across a park road, and on downhill to where a grass track
leads between hedges to the equestrian statue known as the Copper
Horse. Then straight ahead along the Long Walk to the gates of
Windsor Castle. Here turn left into Park Street and then High
Street, then downhill by Thames Street to Windsor Bridge.

ROUTE INBOUND

From Windsor Bridge to the corner of the A30 and Wick Road, Englefield Green $6\frac{1}{2}$ miles (10·5 km)

From Windsor Bridge walk into Windsor up Thames Street and then past the entrance to the castle into the High Street and on into Park Street and thence into Windsor Great Park. Walk away from the castle along the Long Walk to its extremity, and up to the equestrian statue known as the Copper Horse. Continue straight ahead beyond the statue along a grass track between hedges. This leads downhill and then uphill and half left along the side of the palings of Royal Lodge. Cross a park road and take a grass track leading close to the left of Cumberland Lodge, near its tennis court, and on to Cumberland Gate. After passing through Cumberland Gate, turn half left along a grass ride at the edge of Smith's Lawn, which soon passes to the right of Savill Garden. Cross a bridge and walk past the Cumberland Obelisk and on past Obelisk Pond along a park drive. At a crossroads, follow signs for the Totem Pole. At the Totem Pole take the path which leads between upper and lower water and thence leftwards up a long lawn keeping close to a watercourse on the left. Where the lawn ends and a wood bars the way, cross the watercourse and then turn up the first drive to the right. This ride leads on upwards and leftwards to reach an extreme corner of the park at the junction of the A30 and Wick Road.

APPROACH BY CAR

Approach Englefield Green is near Egham in Surrey on the A30 and near the Staines exit of the M25. Windsor is a Royal Borough in Berkshire, on a spur off the M4. **Parking** At Englefield Green, use the Windsor Great Park car park in Wick Road. In Windsor, River Street car park. **Taxis** Windsor: taxi rank (tel. 62020) or Castle Taxis (tel. 61416). Egham: taxi rank (tel. 3195).

APPROACH BY PUBLIC TRANSPORT

Trains British Rail stations at Windsor Central and Windsor Riverside (both by end of Stage). **Buses** Green Line and Alder Valley at Englefield Green (Holly Tree, $\frac{1}{2}$ mile from corner of A30 and Wick Road) and at Windsor (Central Station and High Street).

PUBLIC TRANSPORT FROM END OF STAGE 6

To start of Stage 6 Green Line or Alder Valley, from Windsor to Englefield Green (hourly: journey time 20 minutes). **To start of Stage 5** Train from Windsor Riverside to Staines and change for Weybridge (half-hourly: journey time 1 hour). **To start of Stage 4** Green Line to Hampton Court (half-hourly: journey time 1 hour). **To start of Stage 3** Train from Windsor Riverside to Richmond (half-hourly, hourly on Sundays: journey time 30 minutes).

ACCOMMODATION

Hotels Several hotels in Windsor of which the three principal ones are Castle Hotel, High Street (tel. 51011); Harte and Garter Hotel, High Street (tel. 63426); and Old House Hotel, Thames Street (tel. 61354). **Guest houses and small hotels** Windsor: the William IV Inn, Thames Street (tel. 51004), and several bed-and-breakfasts, among them Mrs Martin's, 34 Dedworth Road (tel. 60876). **Youth Hostel** Edgeworth House, Mill Lane, Windsor (tel. 6170), closed December–February. **Camping** Pomona Farm, Monkey Island Lane, Windsor Road, Bray, Maidenhead, Berkshire – $3\frac{1}{2}$ miles from Windsor and more accessible to Stage 7, open all year; or Sunnybend Farm, Parker's Lane, Maiden's Green, Winkfield Row (tel. 2846) – 4 miles from Windsor or from the Copper Horse, open all year.

REFRESHMENT

Restaurants Bailiwick, Wick Road, Englefield Green; and several in Windsor, among them the Old House by Windsor Bridge. **Snacks** cafeteria in the Savill Garden; and a wide choice at Windsor. **Pubs** The Fox and Hounds, Bishopsgate, and the Adam and Eve, Windsor Thames Street.

TIMES OF ADMISSION

Parks and gardens Windsor Great Park: daylight hours. Savill Garden, daily March–October 10.00–18.00 (till 19.00 in summer). **Houses and museums** Windsor Castle: Precincts, daily 10.00–19.00 May–August, –17.00 March, April, September and October, and –16.00 November–February; including bank holidays. State Apartments: weekdays, 10.30–17.00 in summer and –15.00 in winter, and on summer Sundays 13.00–17.00; but closed during periods of royal residence, usually December and dates in May and June. Frogmore Mausoleum: one day in May, only.

FACILITIES

Tourist information Windsor Central Station (tel. 52010). **Telephone** Cheeseman's Gate, Wick Road. **Toilet** Savill Garden.

DESCRIPTION

Here hills and vales, the woodland and the plain,
Here earth and water, seem to strive again;
Not chaos-like together crushed and bruised,
But, as the world, harmoniously confused:
Where order in variety we see,
And where, though all things differ, all agree.

Alexander Pope, 1688–1744
from 'Windsor Forest'

Like Richmond Park, Windsor Great Park is in origin part of a
medieval forest. But because it is further from London and is
associated with an existing royal palace, it is over twice the size of
Richmond and contains some spectacular landscaping. In fact,
Windsor Great Park is one of the most beautiful examples of the
English style of landscaping, which rejected the Continental fashion
of regimenting nature and instead aimed at adapting it in a subtle
way. What we see as we walk through it is not untamed nature, but
nature as it could have been, completely convincing and yet
contrived, with 'order in variety' throughout. So in it we can at
places happily imagine ourselves in the ancient forest where kings
and princes hunted in a chase whose excitement is so well evoked in
the lines of the ill-fated Henry Howard, son and heir to the Duke of
Norfolk, who was eventually beheaded on the orders of Henry VIII.
Henry Howard wrote of his earlier loose confinement at Windsor
Castle:

The wild forest, the clothéd holts of green,
With reins availed and swift y-breathéd horse,
With cry of hounds, and merry blasts between,
Where we did chase the fearful hart of force.

The Cumberland Obelisk

Here also, according to Malory in *Le Morte d'Arthur*, Sir Launcelot retired for rest and meditation before the jousts arranged for Candlemas to celebrate the admission of Sir Lavaine to the Knights of the Round Table (though his meditation was rudely interrupted by a lady huntress who shot an arrow into his buttock). More prosaically, Windsor Great Park was where Fairfax trained the New Model Army, which was to win the Civil War for the Parliamentarians.

Entering the park through a grove of oaks we walk under beeches and past rhododendrons and soon emerge on a lawn which slopes down to Virginia Water, an artificial lake created in 1750. Royal water parties were held on it in a ceremonial barge, with an accompanying boat carrying a band which played music by Handel, Arne, and other popular composers. The view down the lake from the causeway we cross is superb, with Scots pines prominent along the banks. From this idyllic scene we are confronted by a strange object: a totem pole from British Columbia. It is 100 ft high and made from red cedar 600 years old, and it depicts a genealogical sequence of chiefs, fathers squatting over squatting sons: a real family tree – but without branches! From this we walk through more rhododendrons to a point where a park signpost is placed. The park road down to the right leads the $\frac{1}{4}$ mile to Cheeseman's Gate, at which is the Bailiwick Restaurant.

Meanwhile we continue past the pond named after the Obelisk to the Duke of Cumberland, the militaristic son of George II and commander-in-chief in the Scottish campaign of 1746. Among his lesser appointments he was Ranger of Windsor Park, and under him many of the improvements were made. So, although his obelisk is surmounted by a fiery orb symbolising grenades and cannonballs, it is appropriate that it should rest on a heathery bank and be surrounded by particularly splendid conifers including a lovely Japanese red cedar. Here also is the entrance to the Savill Garden – a recent addition to the attractions of the park – a superb collection of flowering shrubs nurtured in a woodland setting. May and June are the best times to come and see the azaleas and rhododendrons, the magnolias and camellias, in and around the garden: and it also has a cafeteria overlooking the central glade. We can enjoy glimpses of the Savill Garden to the right of our route as we walk on past the obelisk and along the edge of Smith's Lawn, where polo – that sport of princes and South Americans – is often played. And so we come to the Cumberland Gate, at which point we leave Surrey and enter Berkshire (and incidentally join for the remainder of this Stage, and for most of Stages 7 and 8, the London Countryway).

Bishopsgate, ½ mile away from us here, but off our route, can be reached by walking straight along the park road by which we have passed through the Cumberland Gate (or it can also be reached from the Copper Horse by following along or near to the tarmac park route which leads to the right as you stand by the statue and look towards the castle). Bishopsgate is an important bearing point because from it a deviation of 1½ miles beyond leads to the three national monuments associated with Runnymede, where Magna Carta, at once the instrument of baronial privilege and the precursor of our democratic rights, was signed, by the reluctant John in June 1215. For these, leave Windsor Great Park at Bishopsgate and walk along Bishopsgate Road for ¾ mile (passing the Fox and Hounds public house), rejecting a road to the right and to the left. Then at a fork branch left on to Castle Hill Road, which leads to a main road, the A328. Across this, the Royal Air Force Memorial is reached by a marked road leading up Cooper's Hill: the John F. Kennedy memorial and Magna Carta memorial are gained by a public footpath which starts 100 m down the main road to the left, down a drive called Oak Lane. All three monuments are impressive and in good taste, and are dedicated to the ideals expressed by Kennedy as the 'survival and success of liberty'.

After passing through the Cumberland Gate we next traverse a section of woodland which includes, slightly to our right, Coronation Plantation, a rare collection of oaks with specimens from all the countries of the British Commonwealth, planted in 1953. Around us are older oaks and other large trees within the fence of Royal Lodge. In 1815 Shelley, who was living in a house near here at Bishopsgate with Mary Godwin, came into Windsor Park to get colour for his epic poem *Alastor*: 'The oak, expanding its immense and knotty arms, embraces the light beech. The pyramids of the tall cedar over-arching frame most solemn domes within, and far below, like clouds suspended in an emerald sky, the ash and the acacia floating hang, tremulous and pale.'

After this we leave the woods for a grass ride between fields. Ahead is the Copper Horse, and to the right we can see Royal Lodge, rebuilt for George VI when Duke of York, and still lived in by his widow, Queen Elizabeth. It is on the site of a previous Royal Lodge, a Gothick rustic retreat built for George IV when Prince of Wales. A more humble rustic retreat stands in the garden of the present Royal Lodge – Y Bwthyn Bach, a miniature Welsh cottage, built for the present Queen when Princess Elizabeth.

So we come up to the Copper Horse, the equestrian statue of George III, and on reaching it we enjoy the best view in the whole of our Walk, from a vantage point only 75 m high. On a clear day the tall towers of central London can be seen on the horizon to the right, 25 miles away, with the ever-present aircraft climbing and descending at Heathrow in between: and ahead the horizon reveals the hump of Harrow Hill half right and the beginning of the Chiltern Hills around Beaconsfield half left. But the main focus of the view is Windsor Castle, 2½ miles away at the other end of the Long Walk. The Copper Horse was erected to provide a worthy vista from the castle; but the view of the castle from the Copper Horse is far better. 'Towers and battlements it sees, Bosom'd high in tufted trees', in the lines of the youthful Milton, who could see Windsor Castle from a similar distance at his home at Horton (where also he wrote *Lycidas*). To improve the view, it is hard to resist the temptation to scramble up the rusticated stone plinth to where the famous horse with its royal rider, in the garb of a Roman Emperor, is forever striding westwards.

The Long Walk is the creation of Charles II. Although it is out of character with the rest of the Park, in that it is the antithesis of the English style of landscaping, we can readily forgive the regimentation, especially because the King is said to have spent a lot of his time at Windsor walking in the park (and, indeed, had in his escape after the battle of Worcester certainly qualified as a long-distance walker, covering 9 miles in ill-fitting shoes on each of two consecutive nights, fording streams and forcing through thorn hedges): more practically, because the Long Walk serves admirably to link the castle to the park. Originally it was planted with elms,

The Copper Horse in scaffolding

which lasted not far short of 300 years till 1942: they have been replaced with alternate planes and chestnuts which are now growing up well.

As we pace out our 2½ miles along the Long Walk (in normal conditions the grass makes for easier walking than the tarmac) we soon pass on the right high fences behind which a herd of red deer has happily been recently introduced into the park. Their feeding enclosure is near Bear's Rails Gate, whose name denotes an earlier and more cruel form of enclosure, and which is close to Old Windsor and the place where it is believed that the Saxon Kings' manor-house of Windsor (or Windlesore) stood.

Then, after the Long Walk crosses the A308 road, it is bounded to the right by the Home Park, the 'little park under the castle', which is not open to the public. From amongst a group of trees can be discerned the romanesque tower of the Frogmore Mausoleum (1871) where are buried Queen Victoria and Prince Albert. Frogmore features in *The Merry Wives of Windsor* as a place of assignment ('Go through the fields with me to Frogmore,' says the Host of the Garter Inn to Master Caius: 'I will bring thee where Mistress Anne Page is, at a farm-house a-feasting, and thou shalt woo her'), and the scenes in Windsor Park would have occurred in the Home Park around Frogmore. In it was Herne's Oak, traditionally believed to be where Herne the Hunter – a keeper who was wounded by a stag and became insane, tied antlers to his head and ran naked through the forest – hanged himself: and here Shakespeare set the scene of Falstaff's final humiliation.

Finally, at the castle gates, where Wyattville's south front can be well seen, we turn to enter the town of Windsor, and without any intervening modernities are immediately in a sequence of streets which are little changed from the eighteenth century, especially the initial group of houses in Park Street.

In the High Street we pass St John Baptist's, the Windsor parish church, early nineteenth-century: the interior is rather bleak and other than to visit the brass-rubbing centre in the aisle it is enough to notice its west front before moving on to the Windsor Guildhall, an elegant seventeenth-century structure, completed by Wren in

J. R. Cozens: Windsor Castle from the South-west

1690. In the style of several town halls in the Thames Valley, it is open on the ground level – generally an unusual feature in English architecture. The interior columns in this loggia are, surprisingly, disconnected from the ceiling, fulfilling no function.

Just beyond the Guildhall and the ancient Market Cross House next to it, we come to the statue of Queen Victoria and the entrance to Windsor Castle by the Henry VIII gateway, guarded by a policeman without and a guardsman within.

For those who have walked many miles to visit it, and have seen it from afar, the most satisfactory way to enter Windsor Castle is to walk straight through to the North Terrace and there survey the expanse below. There one can appreciate the strategic significance of the castle, perched on an outcrop of chalk and dominating the Thames. In the Thames Valley everything is small-scale; and even this comparatively modest hill of 50 metres above the sea level can stand out as a landmark, visible from 20 miles away, except to the south. Here the Norman conquerors constructed their strong-point as part of a chain of castles encircling London. From it has grown the largest and most historic castle in England.

Because of the extraordinary peacefulness of the Thames Valley during the past 900 years, Windsor Castle has seen scarcely any fighting. It has only twice been besieged – but never taken; both occasions being during the troublesome times of John. It played a part in the manoeuvring between Henry III and Simon de Montfort, and later between Prince Rupert and the Parliamentarians during the Civil War. Otherwise its fortifications have been of use only in keeping in a series of eminent prisoners, including James I of Scotland and Charles I of England.

What is particularly pleasing about the Castle is the sense of continuity. Architecturally, Wyatt and Salvin attempted to recapture the gothic magnificence of Edward III's castle. Likewise, historically, our modern British monarchy is in direct descent from those distant Norman and Plantagenet forebears. The architecture and the institution are really not at all the same as they originally were, but that doesn't seem to matter as we contemplate the Round Tower and the enormous royal standard.

Rather like false teeth, the walls of Windsor are perfected imitations built over ancient foundations. Although the original

Norman keep was of wood, Henry II built extensive stone ramparts, of which portions survive at the base of the Round Tower and in the Winchester Tower (in which Geoffrey Chaucer is thought to have lived when Clerk of the Royal Works at the end of the fourteenth century); and Henry III's buildings can be seen in the three towers facing Windsor Thames Street. Eastwards, the State Apartments and the East and South ranges are mostly the work of James Wyatt (from 1796) and his nephew Sir Jeffrey Wyattville (between 1820–30), built respectively for George III and George IV. Of Charles II's earlier rebuilding, only three rooms remain; they include ceilings by Verrio and wood-carvings by Gibbons, and besides these there is the equestrian statue of Charles II in the Upper Ward. The State Apartments house a great collection of pictures, notably in the Waterloo Chamber the portraits of British and European statesmen and rulers who participated in the defeat of Napoleon; and in other rooms earlier royal portraits including the triple portrait of Charles I by Vandyke. In St George's Hall, the medieval spirit is recaptured within genuinely medieval walls.

But the finest building in the Castle is St George's Chapel, a supreme example of the English perpendicular style of the late fifteenth century. Light and symmetrical, it is a precursor of the Renaissance, with nave and chancel of equal size and significance. Under the marvellous stone vault are to be found a treasure-trove of monuments. The stalls, incredibly intricate and mostly fifteenth-century, are topped with the banners of the present knights and studded with the stall-plates of 700 dead knights. Eleven English kings are buried here, and in the various recesses and around the aisles, tiny chapels and chantries testify to the medieval concern for prayer. St George's Chapel has some of the characteristics of a cathedral, and one of them is that it has maintained a musical tradition, particularly of English cathedral music. There is no better way to appreciate St George's than to attend a choral service, and hear the dulcet tones wafting around the tracery in contrived musical elaboration of much-loved words.

The continuity of Windsor is best expressed in the Order of the Garter. Strangely, at a time when all other important honours are bequeathed only nominally by the Sovereign, the Garter is awarded on her personal decision – an unusual retention (indeed a reinstitution) of a royal prerogative. Men of merit are undoubtedly selected for the honour, but in a world of meritocracy one can sympathise with Lord Melbourne's remark: 'I like the Garter: there's no damned merit in it!' Anyway, the Knights annually proceed to the chapel dressed in all their finery: and so lives on at Windsor in mutated form the cult of Arthur and the Knights of the Grail which inspired Edward III to found the Order in 1348.

Back in Windsor, our route passes beneath the castle down Thames Street. Stage 6 ends at a pedestrian precinct in front of the Old House Hotel, a fine seventeenth-century house supposedly once inhabited by Christopher Wren, which has a large dining-room with extensive views over the river.

SPECIFICS

After passing through nearly a mile of Eton High Street and College, this stage proceeds all the way up the Thames towpath on earth and gravel, easy throughout and traffic-free, passing close by Dorney and Bray.

ROUTE OUTBOUND

From Windsor Bridge to Maidenhead Bridge 7 miles (11 km)

From Windsor bridge walk along Eton High Street as far as Eton College Chapel. Just before the Chapel turn left into Keates Lane: where the main road turns right after 100 m, keep straight ahead along South Meadow Lane, past the Lower Chapel. Later, where this lane takes a sharp left turn, take a lane (tarmac at first, and for pedestrians only) to the right, under the railway and then under the A332 road. Where the lane emerges into an open field, turn left at a footpath sign to the river and then right up the left bank of the Thames (right as you look upstream). The remainder of this Stage is all along the river bank. It leads past Boveney lock, and later under the M4 motorway bridge; past Bray lock, and later under the Maidenhead railway bridge. Here it becomes a short road leading up to the Maidenhead road bridge.

ROUTE INBOUND

From Maidenhead Bridge to Windsor Bridge 7 miles (11 km)

At Maidenhead bridge take the left bank of the Thames downstream, initially by River Road. Always keeping to the towpath, pass under the Maidenhead railway bridge, and later past Bray lock and under the M4 motorway bridge; and further on, past

Boveney lock. ½ mile after Boveney lock, and just before the towpath crosses a side stream of the Thames, leave the towpath along a path leading left at the edge of a large field. 100 m later turn right into a lane. This leads under the A332 road and then under a railway. 100 m later it comes to a road (South Meadow Lane) at a corner. Take the left-hand direction along this lane which leads towards and between college buildings, including the Lower Chapel, to join Keates Lane and continue ahead for 100 m to Eton College Chapel. At this point turn right into Eton High Street and along it to Eton Bridge.

APPROACH BY CAR

Approach At the Windsor end, the Stage is best approached at Eton, adjacent to Windsor. Eton is in Buckinghamshire, off exit 6 of the M4. Maidenhead is in Berkshire, off exits 7 or 9 of the M4. **Parking** At Eton, the Brocas car park at the end of the High Street by Windsor Bridge. At Maidenhead, River Road or other side roads by Maidenhead Bridge.   **Taxis** Slough: Viking Radio Cars (tel. 33193). Maidenhead: Clarke's Taxis (tel. 24323) or Tartan Taxis (tel. 22856 and 21628).

APPROACH BY PUBLIC TRANSPORT

Trains British Rail stations at Windsor Central and Windsor Riverside (both by start of stage) and at Maidenhead (¾ mile from Maidenhead Bridge).   **Buses** Green Line and Alder Valley at Windsor (by Central Station), and Alder Valley and South Midland at Maidenhead bus station (½ mile from Maidenhead Bridge).   **Boat** Salters, at Windsor and Maidenhead (Boulter's Lock).

PUBLIC TRANSPORT FROM END OF STAGE 7

To start of Stage 7 Alder Valley to Windsor Central (every 20 minutes: journey time 34 minutes), or Salters Boat (daily in summer: journey time 2 hours). **To start of Stage 6** Same, then Green Line or Alder Valley from Windsor to Englefield Green (Holly Tree). **To start of Stage 5** Inconvenient. Same as to start of Stage 7 then train from Windsor Riverside to Staines and change for Weybridge (half-hourly: journey time 1 hour). **To start of Stage 4** Same as to start of Stage 7, then Green Line to Hampton Court (half-hourly: journey time 1 hour).

ACCOMMODATION

Hotels For Windsor, see Stage 6. Near Bray: Monkey Island Hotel, Bray, Maidenhead (tel. 23400). **Guest houses and small hotels** For Windsor see Stage 6. Maidenhead: Riviera Hotel (tel. 25425) or Hereward's Guest House (tel. 29038). **Youth hostel** Windsor, see Stage 6. **Group accommodation** Huntercombe Manor, Taplow (Burnham 2716). **Camping** Pomona Farm, Monkey Island Lane, Bray (1 mile from M4 bridge).

REFRESHMENT

Restaurants Eton: the House on the Bridge, the Cockpit. Maidenhead: La Riva (by the bridge). **Snacks** Eton: The Eton Wine Bar. **Pubs** Eton: the Christopher. Dorney: the Pineapple.

TIMES OF ADMISSION

Museums and buildings Windsor Castle: see Stage 6. Eton College: 14.00–17.00 daily in term-time, 10.30–17.00 daily in school holidays. The Brewhouse Gallery, Eton: Saturdays and Sundays 14.30–17.00.

FACILITIES

Tourist Information Windsor Central Station (tel. 52010). Maidenhead Central Library (tel. 25657).

DESCRIPTION

Ye distant spires, ye antique towers,
That crown the watery glade,
Where grateful science still adores
Her Henry's holy shade;
And ye, that from the stately brow
Of Windsor's heights th'expanse below
Of grove, of lawn, of mead survey,
Whose turf, whose shade, whose flowers among
Wanders the hoary Thames along
His silver-winding way.

Thomas Gray, 1716–71
from 'Ode on a Distant Prospect of Eton College'

The iron bridge of 1823 linking Windsor and Eton is now happily
barred to traffic, which releases narrow Eton High Street from an
intolerable burden and enables us to appreciate the charm of its
slightly twisted lines of buildings, now mostly devoted to eating,
drinking and the purchase of antiques. Conspicuous among them is
the Cockpit, former cottages which date from at least 1420. Set back
from the street is St John's, the Eton parish church (nineteenth
century). Then, across Barnes Bridge, we enter the area of the school
and, passing through a group of old houses, with lanes leading off,
we come up to the west front of the chapel and, beyond it, the
entrance to 'School Yard'.

Eton is the most famous of the English 'public' (but really private)
schools, whose demise is constantly predicted but which still flourish;
'*Floreat Etona*' is the school motto. Even those who disapprove of
the system of selection find little to criticise in the way the boys are
taught once there: and the affection felt by Old Etonians for their
school springs in large measure from a youthful appreciation of the

P. Skelton: College and Street, Eton

glorious cluster of buildings that centre on the original school and chapel.

The founder of Eton was Henry VI, and although his intention was secular in so far as he made provision for the education of 70 scholars, it was primarily religious, in the institution of an enormous chapel (designed to be over twice the existing length) dedicated to the Virgin Mary and intended as a place of pilgrimage. The whole project was so closely associated with Henry that when he was deposed in 1461 by the Yorkist Edward IV, Eton College was very nearly annulled. For a long while, the Dean of the Yorkist St George's Chapel and the Provost of the Lancastrian Eton Chapel squabbled over relics, grants and other royal and aristocratic favours: fortunately, they have both survived the vicissitudes of five hundred years, and still face each other from a mere half-mile distance.

Eton Chapel, though not as intricate or well-furnished as St George's (though with impressive medieval wall-paintings), presents a larger, higher, unencumbered space; and with a new stone vault and bright new eastern windows the visual impact from under the organ loft is very striking. In the school yard, the north side (Lower School) is fifteenth-century, the east side (Lupton's Tower and range) is sixteenth-century, and the west side (Upper School) is seventeenth century. Lupton's Tower is reminiscent of the entrance towers to St James's Palace and Hampton Court. The best way for a quick circuit of the college buildings (if they are open) is to proceed under Lupton's Tower through to the cloisters, and then keep bearing left, past the Provost's garden, with a view of the playing fields, and then back through Weston's Yard to regain the Long Walk at the main entrance of Upper School. At weekends, the Brewhouse Gallery should not be missed: it contains a large collection of prints and pictures in which the rustic pre-industrial age presents itself for our inspection.

After Henry VI the greatest royal patron of the college was George III; not in material terms but in the interest he took in it, especially when living at Windsor Castle. Eton still celebrates his birthday on the fourth of June, and Etonians still wear black tail-coats of the style which was worn when the school went into mourning at his death. This royal patronage, together with a convenient distance from London, combined to make Eton the pre-eminent upper-class school, as testified by twenty Old Etonian Prime Ministers, including Walpole, Chatham, Wellington, Melbourne, Gladstone, Salisbury and more recently Eden, Douglas-Home and Macmillan. Amongst famous rebels have been Shelley, Swinburne and Eric Blair – better known as George Orwell. And Lord Milford, an Old Etonian, has for many years been the only overt communist in either of the Houses of Parliament.

We leave Eton between the Lower Chapel and the music school, on which the inscription $\theta \epsilon o \varsigma \ \Omega \pi \alpha \sigma \epsilon \ \theta \epsilon \sigma \pi \iota \nu \ A \iota o \delta \eta \nu$ means 'The god bestowed the divine song' – a quotation from Homer. After leaving Eton, and just before passing under the railway bridge, a backward look reveals the classic view of Windsor Castle in all its complexity, with the Curfew tower and its steep French-style roof (emulated from Viollet-le-duc's restorations at Carcassone) glowering at us across the Brocas – a meadow named after one of the original burgher families of Windsor. Soon after, we reach the Thames and remain on the towpath for the remainder of this Stage. It is throughout in Buckinghamshire, and in a district known as the Chiltern Hundreds. These were lands anciently held by the Crown. The office of Steward became a sinecure during the early eighteenth century and is still used, not for any monetary reward, but as a convenient device for members of the House of Commons who wish to vacate their seats: by 'applying for the Chiltern Hundreds', they in effect disqualify themselves as Members of Parliament.

Here we see a Thames distinctly different from when we left it 15 miles back at the end of Stage 4 – now narrower and more congested. In summer, particularly at weekends, the constant drone of motor-cruisers destroys the peacefulness of the river. Fortunately for us, they are ultimately limited in movement by the capacity of the locks, so that after a convoy of half-a-dozen or so there is relative quiet till the next convoy. More admirable to walkers are the oarsmen, and on this stretch in term-time we may see the Etonians maintaining an aquatic tradition of 150 years in their riggers, pairs, fours or eights. Best of all is to see the Eton eight, distinguished on special occasions by their light blue blades and braids, striking in unison with apparent effortlessness and swinging together with their 'bodies between their knees', as in the accurate

but arresting refrain of their famous boating song.

Sport and leisure are now the chief usages of the middle and upper Thames, but it was not always so. The Thames, until the coming of the railways, was a great highway for trade. Early man, traces of whose settlements of around 3,000 BC have been found at Bray, is known to have used dug-out canoes and skin-covered coracles; and later came punts and barges of increasing size and efficiency. From the Middle Ages, they carried downstream to London wool, hides, cheese, meat, cereals, hay, wood and stone. And, as trade developed, the smaller but as valuable upstream flow consisted of cloth and manufactured products. The trade reached its peak in the early nineteenth century, when large barges with capacity for 130 tons got from Oxford to London in $3\frac{1}{2}$ days on the average and earned as much as £50 for the trip. The trade was linked to the West of England at Reading by means of the Kennet and Avon canal, and to the Midlands at Oxford by the Oxford canal.

Boveney lock is distinguished by rollers – on which small boats can be handled without having to use the lock: an eminently sensible arrangement which we only encounter next at Iffley in Stage 14. A little beyond it we pass the chapel of St Mary Magdalen, a tiny church with several thirteenth-century portions, by origin probably a 'chapel of ease' to Boveney Court close by. An old brick house 150 m behind the chapel has latticed windows and fine chimneys. Just after the chapel we pass Andrews' boathouse, where the Eton College eights are housed. The ensuing stretch of river up to Bray lock is pleasant enough on our bank, but the further bank bears some less rustic features – a caravan site, a marina and, later, a pulp-mill.But on the credit side I definitely put Down Place, surely the most extravagant of all Thames riverside villas, featuring a ruined tower and great mullioned windows and ivy-covered walls, gloomy and dramatic in appearance, and not surprisingly frequently used for film sets. It is framed by a fine arrangement of evergreens – Wellingtonias, cedars, yew, monkey-puzzles and holly – and is preceded by a line of tall poplars and matched on our bank by a grove of chestnuts.

Windsor Castle from the Brocas

The little island that soon follows is Queen's Eyot, owned by Eton College, and a point at which Etonians can disembark and rest from rowing. 100 m upstream from Queen's Eyot a channel joins the Thames on the further bank; and opposite it, on our side, just after we get our final view of Windsor Castle in the distance, a footpath leads off to the right for ½ mile to Dorney. A diversion here will lead us to St James's, an exquisite little flint church, basically of the thirteenth century with a sixteenth-century red-brick tower. This church is rich in furnishings – Norman font, seventeenth-century pews, gallery and pulpit – and has a fine Elizabethan tomb to William and Elizabeth Garrard. It stands next to Dorney Court, which for centuries has been owned by the Palmer family and contains an original hall of around 1500, with much panelling and many family portraits. The house can be seen by appointment. The famous gardener, Rose, who presented the first pineapple to be grown in England to Charles II, supervised horticulture at Dorney Court for Sir Philip Palmer, and the pineapple motif is much in evidence; the local pub is 'The Pineapple'. Altogether, Dorney is well worth its ½ mile diversion, a secluded haven in marked contrast to the rush of the nearby motorway and flightpath, and to all the thousands who on them daily post over land and ocean without rest.

A second island (or eyot) appears shortly thereafter. This is Monkey Island, so called because in the original fishing lodge built in the early eighteenth century, the French artist Andien de Clermont depicted exotic scenes with monkeys dressed in the height of fashion as ladies and gentlemen of the day, and indulging in sporting pastimes – fishing, shooting and boating. These charming paintings are still preserved within the structure of the present hotel, and the little island is also graced by an eighteenth-century building in the form of a temple, built for the third Duke of Marlborough. Monkey Island Hotel is one of the most luxurious hostelries on our route, and is very attractively situated, though well within the sound-band of the M4 motorway.

300 m upstream we pass under the M4 motorway bridge, on which the planners have commendably supplied pedestrian crossings over the river, providing the opportunity to reach the further bank. Those wanting to visit the Monkey Island Hotel or the Bray camping site in Monkey Island Lane should cross by the

downstream side of the Bridge: those going to Bray village or
church, by the upstream side. The hotels of Monkey Island or Bray
involve no more than ¾ mile deviation: but campers should be
warned that the Pomona camping site is rather further (over ¾ mile
down Monkey Island Lane) and has only limited capacity.

After passing under the M4 motorway we soon come to Bray
lock, at which there is no crossing, and after it we get a good view of
the ensemble of village houses and St Michael's church, externally
mostly fifteenth-century, with a fine tower. It is famous for the
legend of the Vicar of Bray, the prototype of placemen. The
apocryphal story was originally told (in Fuller's *Worthies of England*
published in 1662) of a vicar who was the incumbent here in the
sixteenth century:

> The vivacious vicar hereof, living under King Henry the Eighth,
> King Edward the Sixth, Queen Mary, and Queen Elizabeth, was
> first a Papist, then a Protestant, then a Papist, then a Protestant
> again. He had seen some martyrs burnt (two miles off) at Windsor,
> and found this fire too hot for his tender temper. This Vicar,
> being taxed by one for being a turncoat, and an inconsistent
> changeling, 'Not so,' said he, 'for I always kept my principle,
> which is this – to live and die the Vicar of Bray.'

The story was later applied to the equally upsetting times of the
seventeenth century, starting 'In good King Charles's golden reign';
but the real force of the legend is that it applies eternally, not just to
timorous vicars, but to people we all know!

From Bray to the end of the Stage a continuous succession of
houses lines the further bank. It is amusing to speculate on the
inspiration of the various architectural styles, some of them (with
slatted wooden shutters, or surrounding first-floor veranda, or
ornate balcony) being clearly suitable for climates much hotter and
sunnier than that of the Thames valley.

Finally, a straight stretch of ½ mile leads up to the Maidenhead
railway bridge. This remarkable structure was designed by I. K.
Brunel, the youthful chief engineer of the Great Western Railway, in
1838. It is built entirely of brick and has the widest span (128 ft) and
shallowest arch (24 ft) yet achieved in pure brick construction. A

plaque commemorates his design, and under the bridge a good
shout will produce an exciting resonance. Turner used this bridge as
the scene for his extraordinary painting 'Rain, Steam and Speed',
showing an early GWR engine rushing across it at the then amazing
speed of 60 miles an hour (nowadays 125 mph is attained).
Incidentally, although the railways ruined the trading economy of
the Thames, they indirectly preserved much of it from
industrialisation: and so we should not grudge the two railway
bridges – or indeed the two motorway bridges – which we pass
under in this Stage and which sweep untold numbers across the river
at high speeds, leaving to us the true appreciation of it.

Maidenhead rail and road bridges

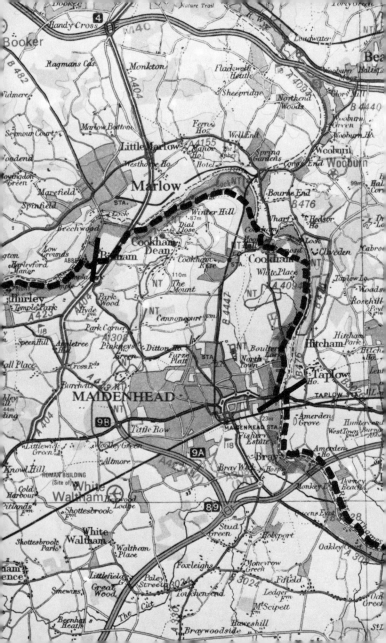

SPECIFICS

The first half of this Stage is mostly up the bank of the Thames, beginning on a pavement but deteriorating to gravel and then some muddy patches before reaching Cookham. The second half very soon leaves the river and proceeds up Winter Hill by grassy tracks and then down the far side through beech-woods. Of the whole Stage, less than a mile is beside traffic.

ROUTE OUTBOUND

From Maidenhead Bridge to the Bisham War Memorial 7 miles (11 km)

(a) From Maidenhead Bridge to Cookham Church 3 miles (5 km)
At Maidenhead Bridge go up the right bank of the Thames (left as you look upstream) along a pavement and then embankment beside Ray Mead Road to Boulters Lock. Shortly after, leave the road to follow the towpath along the Cliveden reach. Where this ceases, at a former ferry point, turn left along a path near the edge of a wood. The path soon proceeds parallel and to the left of a private driveway, and, just after Mill House, it joins Mill Lane. At the end of Mill Lane, turn right along Sutton Road into Cookham village. Continuing on Sutton Road after it passes the High Street, go round a corner and then left into Church Approach. Cross the churchyard to the left of the church.

(b) From Cookham Church to the Bisham War Memorial 4 miles (6 km)
From Cookham Church, walk through the churchyard to the river and walk upstream for over $\frac{1}{4}$ mile round a bend in the river. Just before the towpath goes over a bridge, turn left across a meadow to a gate leading to a farm track. Cross the farm track and further hedge, and then turn right along the edge of a golf course. The

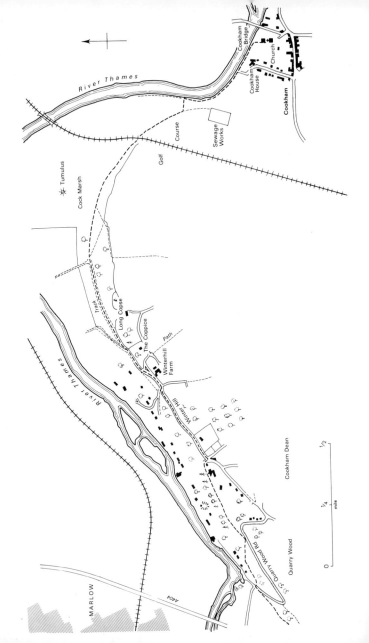

footpath then leads under a railway bridge, where we leave the golf-course path and proceed ahead along a track leading slightly right and down into Cockmarsh. The track continues along the bottom of the hill, then slopes upwards and emerges at the top by Winter Hill Farm. Turn right along the road, ignoring two lanes leading down to the right, to reach the vantage point of Winter Hill. Beyond the hilltop open space, turn right in front of Dial Place and enter a narrow signposted path that passes to the right of the entrance to a house named 'Rivendell'. This path, which as far as Bisham-under-Wood is waymarked by white arrows, leads through beech-woods. At a fork bear right. The path then leads up to a road (Quarry Wood Road) but, without crossing the road, turns downhill by a steep path to cross it lower down at a corner. Then continue along a signposted path along the lower edge of the wood, keeping parallel to a stream. The path leads to the cottages of Bisham-under-Wood, and then crosses the A404 to a small lane which leads to a road junction at the wayside crucifix war memorial in Bisham.

ROUTE INBOUND

From the Bisham War Memorial to Maidenhead Bridge 7 miles (11 km)

(a) From the Bisham War Memorial to Cookham Church 4 miles (6 km)

At the crucifix war memorial at Bisham, turning away from the village, take a small dead-end lane to the left which soon peters out and leads to a path which crosses the A404 to the cottages of Bisham-under-Wood. Pass between the cottages to a path leading leftwards and then left again along the lower edge of Quarry Wood, parallel and to the right of a stream. This path is waymarked with white arrows as far as Winter Hill. After $\frac{3}{4}$ mile it comes to a road (Quarry Wood Road) which it crosses, and then leads uphill, soon becoming steep. Where it comes up to meet the road again, take a path to the left, which contours through the wood and then leads beside a fence to emerge at a road in front of Dial Place. Here turn left along the road, past the vantage point of Winter Hill. Less than

½ mile further on, opposite Winter Hill Farm, turn obliquely left down an unpaved road marked as National Trust property. This lane leads downhill and then continues along the lower edge of the hill beside Cockmarsh. It then mounts slightly and leads under a railway. Immediately afterwards, take the footpath on the right which leads along the edge of a golf course for about 200 m: then turn left at a stile and across a farm track and then across a meadow to the river, just downstream of a towpath bridge. At the river, turn right and follow the towpath downstream as far as Cookham church.

(b) From Cookham Church to Maidenhead Bridge: 3 miles (5 km) From Cookham Church walk through the churchyard to Church Approach and thence right into Sutton Road. This leads round a corner and passes Cookham High Street. Continue along Sutton Road, then left into Mill Lane. Before Mill House follow a signposted path along a belt of wood, parallel to a driveway. The path leads to the river at a former ferry point. Here turn right and follow the right bank of the Thames downstream. This eventually joins a road (Ray Mead Road) which leads to Boulters Lock and then continues downstream to Maidenhead bridge.

APPROACH BY CAR

Approach Maidenhead is in Berkshire, off exits 7 or 9 of the M4. Cookham is on the A4049 north of Maidenhead. Bisham is 1 mile from Marlow, which lies off the A404 which links the M4 and the M40. **Parking** At Maidenhead, in small roads near the bridge over the Thames. At Cookham, in or near Church Approach. At Bisham, in the dead-end lane by the war memorial. **Taxis** Maidenhead: Clarke's Taxis (tel. 24323) or Tartan Taxis (tel. 22856 or 21628). Cookham: Cookham Taxis (Bourne End 20380). Marlow: Marlow Taxis (tel. 3955).

APPROACH BY PUBLIC TRANSPORT

Trains British Rail stations at Maidenhead ($\frac{3}{4}$ mile from
Maidenhead Bridge) and Marlow ($1\frac{1}{4}$ mile from Bisham War
Memorial).   **Buses** Alder Valley and South Midland at
Maidenhead bus station ($\frac{1}{2}$ mile from Maidenhead Bridge) and
Alder Valley at Marlow (Quoitings Square).   **Boats** Salters' Boats
at Maidenhead and Marlow.

PUBLIC TRANSPORT FROM END OF STAGE 8

To start of Stage 8 Train from Marlow to Maidenhead (hourly,
none on Sundays, journey time 25 minutes). Or Alder Valley bus
from Marlow to Maidenhead (hourly weekdays and two-hourly
Sundays, journey time 40 minutes). Or Salters' Boats (daily in
summer, journey time 2 hours).   **To start of Stage 7** Alder Valley
bus from Marlow to Maidenhead as above; then from Maidenhead
station to Windsor Central (every 20 minutes, journey time 34
minutes). Or Salters' Boats (daily in summer, journey time
$3\frac{3}{4}$ hours).   **To start of Stage 6** Inconvenient, but attainable as for
start of Stage 7, then Green Line or Alder Valley from Windsor
Central to Englefield Green (Holly Tree).   **To start of Stage 5** No
convenient public transport.

ACCOMMODATION

Hotels Near Maidenhead (along Stage 7): Monkey Island Hotel,
Bray, Maidenhead (tel. 23400). Marlow: The Compleat Angler
(tel. 4444).   **Guest houses and small hotels** Maidenhead: see Stage 7,
also Boulters Lock Inn (tel. 21291). Bourne End: Old Forge Guest
House, Well End (tel. 20619). Marlow: George & Dragon
(tel. 3887).

REFRESHMENT

Restaurants Maidenhead: La Riva (by the bridge). Cookham: the Bell and Dragon. Bisham: The Bull. **Snacks** Boulters Lock. **Pubs** Cookham: The King's Arms. Bisham: The Bull.

TIMES OF ADMISSION

Parks and Gardens Cliveden Gardens: year round, daily except Mondays and Tuesdays, 11.00–18.30 including bank holidays. **Houses and Museums** Stanley Spencer Gallery, Cookham: April– October 10.30–13.00 and 14.00–18.00, and winter weekends 11.00–13.00 and 14.00–17.00.

FACILITIES

Tourist information Maidenhead Central Library (tel. 25657).

DESCRIPTION

There is a hill beside the silver Thames,
Shady with birch and beech and odorous pine:
And brilliant underfoot with thousand gems
Steeply the thickets to his floods decline.
    Straight trees in every place
    Their thick tops interlace,
And pendant branches trail their foliage fine
    Upon his watery face.

Robert Bridges, 1844–1930

Maidenhead (whose old centre is $\frac{3}{4}$ mile west of the bridge) does not
figure prominently in history, though the bridge has always been of
importance: in 1400 it was held for some time by the Duke of
Surrey and other rebels against the vanguard of Henry IV's army. It
acquired its greatest fame as a fashionable weekend resort earlier in
this century. Skindles Hotel on the opposite bank was once a centre
of gaiety, as was also the former Guards' Boat Club just below the
bridge. Very appropriately, the barge of Jesus College Oxford,
beautifully repaired thanks to a local benefactor, has been moved to
Maidenhead and is worth examining, especially since the few
remaining barges at Oxford cannot be so closely seen from our
route.

    Boulters Lock is much visited, partly because of the restaurant
and gardens on the island beyond it, approached by a bridge over
the lock. A boulter is a long fishing-line with many hooks, such as
might have been used here in the past. Nowadays fishing on the
Thames is a small-scale affair, conducted by individualists who seek
a few hours of peace and quiet, rather than the expectation of a
large catch. At weekends they take up their pitches at close intervals

Cliveden, house and reach

along the towpath, sometimes with quite elaborate equipment, and
in most months enduring the cold weather in solitary vigil. On these
reaches they most commonly catch dace and gudgeon. But at the
locks the full range of permitted fish is listed: Barbel, Bleak, Bream,
Carp, Chub, Dace, Flounders, Gudgeon, Perch, Pike, Roach, Rudd,
Tench and Trout. To these may eventually be added Salmon, as
explained in Stage 4.

After Boulters Lock comes a 1½ mile stretch where on the other
bank 'there is a hill beside the silver Thames'. This, apart from
Windsor, is our first contact with the chalk formations which
westwards form the Chilterns, and which here bar the Thames from
flowing east and force it to the south. Below Maidenhead, the soil
has been of gravel and clay, formations from the comparatively
recent Eocene and Palaeocene periods, and unconducive to
variations in altitude: above Maidenhead in Stages 8–12 we
encounter small but distinctive hills of the older chalk which add
such charm and character to the scenery. The hill we pass here is
particularly impressive, with its steep command of the Thames; so it
is not surprising to learn that besides being the site for a great house
at Cliveden in recent centuries, it also (at its southern end near
Taplow) was the site of a Saxon burial mound of AD 620, in which
was discovered one of the best Anglo-Saxon collections in England,
now in the British Museum.

On our side of the river the ground is still flat, and the towpath is
pleasantly encased in bushes and trees, including some tall poplars.
To our left are old iron railings, of a type much more common
before World War II, when most were melted down for munitions.
Beyond them is an attractive house, White Place. On the other side
are the beech-woods, which give way to lawns and gardens just by
My Lady Ferry, where formerly the towpath changed banks. These
are the lower gardens of Cliveden House, an enormous Italianate
mansion (1849, Barry) which can be discerned on top of the hill
from the Maidenhead end of the reach. The gardens are open to the
public but have to be approached from over Cookham Bridge,
unless we can persuade a boat to take us across at My Lady Ferry.
The house was owned for most of this century by the Astor family.
The first Lord Astor was a New York multi-millionaire who took up
residence in England; his son and daughter-in-law (Nancy Astor,

the first woman MP) in the 1930s took a strong political line against confrontation with Nazi Germany, and they and their circle were known as the Cliveden Set. At the time of his grandson, the third Lord Astor, Cliveden once again became front-page news as the scene of assignation in the Profumo scandal, which rocked the government of Harold Macmillan in 1963. The ornate cottage furthest downstream from the ferry-point was where the ill-fated Stephen Ward held his parties. Scandal also attached to an earlier great house at Cliveden, when owned by George Villiers, second Duke of Buckingham. This 'lord of useless thousands' exercised a powerful and unpredictable influence at the court of Charles II: and his violent private life included the seduction of the wife of the Duke of Shrewsbury, and the murder of her husband in a duel. As a musical footnote to Cliveden, it was here at a masque in 1740 that Thomas Arne's 'Rule Britannia' was first performed.

At My Lady Ferry we leave the river bank for the rest of the Stage: but after a short while we pass a former mill, which is on a side stream of the Thames in an area where the river divides into several channels, designed to ease navigation as well as to feed the water-mill. These mills required a constant supply of water to turn the wheels and so from early medieval times the millers constructed weirs to block the flow of the river. So as to enable boats to pass, the centre of the weir had a removable section of log or tackle, known as a flash lock. When it was removed, a large volume of water flooded downstream, lowering the level of the upper reach by several inches for perhaps a couple of miles upstream. The downstream boats rode the flash in swift though sometimes hazardous speed. When the flash had reduced the difference between the two levels, the upstream boats would be either poled or winched up through the flash lock, the winch being situated some hundreds of feet upstream from the weir, on the river-bank. This whole procedure could in theory be mutually beneficial to millers and to boat-owners, but the trouble was that the millers used it for their own ends, taking little account of the boat traffic movements, proliferating their mills and weirs, and generally charging exorbitant fees for flashing the locks. Meanwhile, at other points on the river, temporary structures were constantly erected for catching fish. Local quarrels escalated. Clause 33 of Magna Carta of 1215 states '*omnes*

kidelli deponantur' ('all the weirs shall be put down'); and in 1252
Parliament enacted against river obstructions. In 1472 an Act of
Edward IV refers to the 'laudable statute of magna carta' and
forbids any improvements to existing 'weirs, fishgarths, locks,
ebbing-weirs, kedels, becks or floodgates'. But it is evident that these
medieval statutes were never effectively promulgated; and it was not
until the advent of the pound locks that these reaches of the Thames
were properly cleared of obstructions, and the millers mostly
relegated to smaller streams.

After passing the entrance to Formosa House, built for Admiral
Sir George Young in 1785, we proceed into Cookham. This ancient
village formed part of the dowry of the Queens of England from
Edward I's reign to Henry VIII's and, as so often, our visual link
with those early times is to be found in the church – Holy Trinity –
which comprises a Norman wall and window in the nave and
thirteenth-century walls and arches in the nave and aisles. The tower
dates from 1500. The medieval spirit is also exemplified at Cookham
church by the Lady Chapel, on the site of which an anchoress, or
female hermit, lived in the twelfth century, supported by alms from
the local community and from Henry II himself. There are also
medieval tiles within the altar rails. The village has retained several
eighteenth-century buildings, particularly those close to the church, of
which Tarry Stone House is the finest. This is named after a sarsen
stone – a 'vagrant' forced into the locality by ice-age glaciation, and
placed in the village by some early inhabitants. Cookham is also
renowned through its local artist, Stanley Spencer (1891–1959),
some of whose works are in the church and in a gallery in the High
Street. His strange balloon-like figures are set in easily recognisable
local scenes, most remarkably in the unfinished canvas of 'Christ
preaching at Cookham Regatta'.

From Cookham we pass across open pasturage and thence under
a railway into Cockmarsh, now owned and preserved by the
National Trust. In it to the right we can see four barrows, or burial
mounds, of which two have been identified as early Bronze Age. And
so on up to the summit of Winter Hill, from which we get a fine
panorama to the north, which is shared by many others from their

Stanley Spencer: View from Cookham Bridge

cars. The final section of Stage 8 (which is throughout in Berkshire) begins mysteriously down a narrow path and then for $1\frac{1}{4}$ miles is through beech-woods. Beeches, together with oaks, are the dominant forest-formers of the temperate regions of the world, and covered much of the Thames valley before the advent of man. Contemplation of this may help to distract us from the man-made sounds of motor-traffic, which become increasingly strident as we come close to and cross the A404. Admirers of *The Wind in the Willows* will want to know that Kenneth Grahame completed that masterpiece when living at Cookham Dean, near Winter Hill. So in these woods we may imagine his four archetypal characters – Ratty, Mole, Badger and Toad. The first three will, I hope, be walking the Thames Valley Heritage Walk; but Toad, I fear, will be racing along the A404 in his high-powered car, not without feelings of disdain for the humble pedestrians.

This road has had the bad effect of isolating the charming group of cottages of Bisham-under-Wood. But to its credit we can at least attribute a new bridge over the Thames. For walkers wishing to make direct for Marlow, an alternative to going through Bisham is to leave our route at the point where it crosses Quarry Wood road (at which point the London Countryway also finally leaves us); take this road to the right; climb up on to the A404 by means of the steps placed there by the local Ramblers Association; thence across the Thames and so upstream by the left bank into Marlow. From here our route can be regained by walking a mile along the road from Marlow bridge to the end of the Stage at the Bisham war memorial.

Stage 8 has much to offer in variety and attractive features, with Cookham as a splendid half-way halt. At the end of it, through walkers will have completed half the Thames Valley Heritage Walk.

The beech wood on Winter Hill

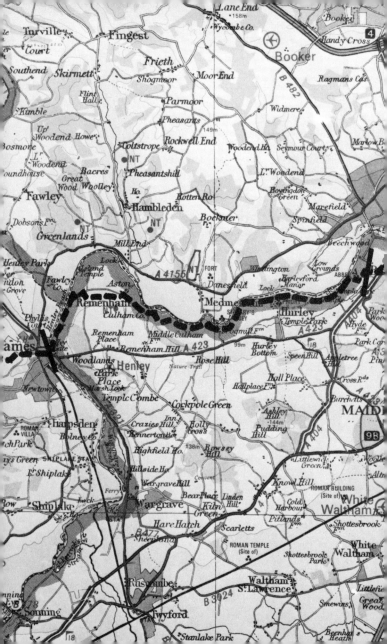

SPECIFICS

4 miles of this Stage are along the Thames towpath, but the remainder – between Bisham and Hurley and between Culham and Remenham – are slightly away from the river (1 mile on roads). There is soft going around Temple Mills and Culham. The route leads throughout through very pleasant scenery, and passes by the sites of three former abbeys.

ROUTE OUTBOUND

From the Bisham War Memorial to Henley Bridge 7½ miles (11·5 km)

(a) From the Bisham War Memorial to Hurley Lock 2 miles (3 km)
At the Bisham crucifix war memorial, take a lane signposted to Temple. Temple Lane leads around Bisham Abbey to the river and then on to Temple Mills. Here, where the lane turns away left, keep straight on past new houses and then a row of cottages, ignoring a 'No Through Road' sign, to a signposted footpath at the far end. This leads through woods, at one point going through a tunnel under a small road. After passing through a gate at the start of a surfaced farm road, turn right on to a short signposted footpath to reach the river, and then turn left up the towpath. At the entrance to Hurley Lock cut, cross rightwards by a wooden footbridge and walk up to the lock.

(b) From Hurley Lock to Henley Bridge 5½ miles (8·5 km)
At Hurley Lock walk upstream and regain the right bank of the Thames (left as you look upstream) by a footbridge. Continue up the towpath, past riverside houses at Frogmill, and later passing Medmenham Abbey on the further bank. Then cross a stile on to a riverside footpath through fields. Five further stiles follow this stile. At the fifth, the path veers away from the river (you have gone too

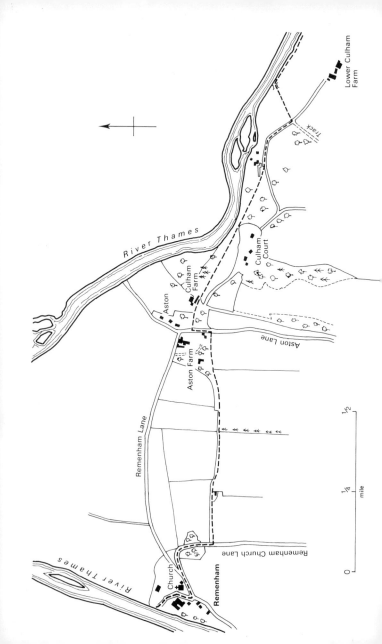

River Thames

Lower Culham
Farm

Track

River Thames

Culham
Court

Culham
Farm

Aston

Aston Lane

Aston Farm

Remenham Lane

Remenham Church Lane

Church

Remenham

0   ¼   ½
          mile

far beside the river if you come to a fence without a stile, near the downstream end of an island) and leads half left and diagonally across a field to a junction of farm roads. Turn along the right-hand track to where it bends left uphill after passing farm buildings on the right. Where the track leaves these buildings, leave it and go straight ahead on to a waymarked right of way through a farm gate. The route leads for 100 m to the corner of an enclosure, and then contours across a field and through stiles and gates between the grounds of Culham Court to the left and the river to the right. The right of way then goes through the middle of a long field to a signposted gate, passing to the left of Holme Farm down a tarmac lane. At end, turn left up lane for 100 m, then, just past Highway Cottage, turn right up a footpath along the edge of a field, which leads on to a farm track which continues straight ahead through fields for $\frac{1}{2}$ mile. At a tarmac lane, turn right and follow it down and round to Remenham Church. Just past the church bear right as far as where the tarmac ceases, then over a stile to rejoin the river. Turn left and follow the towpath upstream to Henley Bridge.

ROUTE INBOUND

From Henley Bridge to the Bisham War Memorial $7\frac{1}{2}$ miles (11·5 km)

(a) From Henley bridge to Hurley Lock $5\frac{1}{2}$ miles (8·5 km)
At Henley Bridge cross to the right bank of the Thames and walk downstream along the towpath for 1 mile as far as the red-brick houses of Remenham, close beside the river and $\frac{1}{4}$ mile upstream from Temple Island. Turn right by a stile into Remenham, and along a lane: immediately after passing the church turn left and then 100 m on, fork right. The lane leads uphill and into a copse: at the top of the rise and beyond the copse, turn left on to a footpath along a farm track through fields. $\frac{1}{2}$ mile later, where this farm track turns left, continue straight ahead across a stile and downhill along the edge of a field to join a lane just by Highway Cottage. Here turn left for 100 m, then right, up a tarmac driveway leading to Holme Farm. Passing to the right of Holme Farm, enter a field at a footpath signpost and contour across the field and through gates

and stiles between Culham Court on the right and the river on the left. The right of way then continues across a further field at much the same level, to the upper corner of an enclosure, from which it leads on to join a farm track. Follow this farm track downhill to the right of farm buildings. At a point where another farm track joins from the right, enter a field on the left and cross it diagonally to the left to the far corner. Here the route regains the river bank and continues down it, past Medmenham Abbey on the farther bank, then past riverside houses at Frogmill and on to Hurley lock, which is approached across a wooden footbridge.

(b) From Hurley Lock to the Bisham War Memorial 2 miles (3 km)
At Hurley lock walk downstream and regain the right bank of the Thames by a wooden footbridge; then downstream along the river bank along a field and along the edge of a wood. The right of way turns away from the river and into the wood. 200 m later, after a stile, turn left at a signposted path through a gate and then through woods, at one point going through a tunnel under a small road, and on through housing at Temple Mills. Straight ahead along a lane which leads past a marina and then towards and around Bisham Abbey where it joins another road at the Bisham crucifix war memorial.

APPROACH BY CAR

Approach Bisham is in Berkshire, 1 mile from Marlow, which lies off the A404 which links the M4 and M40. Hurley is off the A423, between Marlow and Henley. Henley-on-Thames is in Oxfordshire, 8 miles north of Reading, at the junction of the A423 and A4155.
Parking At Bisham, in the dead-end lane by the war memorial. At Hurley, at car park near church. At Henley, car park off Market Place.   **Taxis** Marlow: Marlow Taxis (tel. 3955). Henley: Henley Taxis (tel. 4937), or Mick's Taxis (tel. 3482).

APPROACH BY PUBLIC TRANSPORT

Trains British Rail Stations at Marlow ($1\frac{1}{4}$ miles from Bisham War Memorial) and Henley ($\frac{1}{4}$ mile from Henley Bridge). **Buses** Alder Valley at Marlow (West Street) and Henley (Hart Street/New Street); and Oxford South Midland at Henley.

PUBLIC TRANSPORT FROM END OF STAGE 9

To start of Stage 9 Alder Valley bus from Henley to Marlow (hourly, journey time 25 minutes). **To start of Stage 8** Train from Henley to Maidenhead (hourly, none on winter Sundays, journey time 40 minutes, changing at Twyford): or Oxford South Midland bus, from Henley to Maidenhead (every 2 hours, journey time 25 minutes). **To start of Stage 7** Train from Henley to Windsor (hourly, not on winter Sundays, journey time $1\frac{1}{4}$ hours, changing at Twyford and Slough). Or Oxford South Midland bus from Henley to Maidenhead (every 2 hours, journey time 40 minutes) and then Alder Valley to Windsor (every 20 minutes, journey time 35 minutes). **To start of Stage 6** Inconvenient: but as above, then Green Line or Alder Valley from Windsor to Englefield Green.

ACCOMMODATION

Hotels Marlow: the Compleat Angler (tel. 4444). Hurley: the Old Bell Inn (Littlewick Green 4244). Henley: the Red Lion (tel. 2161). **Guest Houses and small hotels** Marlow: George and Dragon (tel. 3887). Henley: Thamesmead (tel. 4745); the Little White Hart Hotel, Riverside (tel. 4145). **Youth Hostels** Henley: Friends' Meeting House, Northfield End (tel. 2060) closed January–March, and Thamesfield Residential Youth Centre (tel. 2276). **Camping** Hurley: Frogmill Camping Site (Littlewick Green 3501). Henley: Swiss Farm (tel. 3205). Both open March–October.

REFRESHMENT

Restaurant Bisham: the Bull. **Snacks** Henley: Fleur de Lys and
Tearooms. **Pubs** The Bull, Bisham; the Rising Sun, Hurley; the
Flower Pot, Aston; the Old White Hart, Henley.

FACILITIES

Telephones Temple; Hurley; Aston. **Toilet** Henley, Town Hall.

DESCRIPTION

The Childe departed from his father's hall:
It was a vast and venerable pile;
So old, it seeméd only not to fall,
Yet strength was pillar'd in each massy aisle.
Monastic dome! condemned to uses vile!
Where superstition once had made her den
Now Paphian girls were known to sing and smile;
And monks might deem their time was come again
If ancient tales say true, nor wrong these holy men.

Byron, 1788–1824
from 'Childe Harold's Pilgrimage'

The war memorial at Bisham lies at the end of the village. Standing by it, the most noticeable building is an enormous brick-covered windowless structure, whose anonymity provokes curiosity. The answer is obtained a few metres towards the village where a grandiose entrance proclaims the Central Council of Physical Recreation at Bisham Abbey. From this entrance through the trees can be glimpsed Bisham Abbey itself: but that is as near as one can get, since visitors are not admitted (except by written appointment). It is curious to reflect that a house built originally for prayer should end up now as a centre for sport, where girls are indeed known to sing and smile, but which is now even more closed to the public than any monastery was!

The foundation graduated from a Templar preceptory to an Augustinian priory, and then a Benedictine abbey. Richard Neville, Earl of Warwick – the 'Kingmaker' – was buried here after his hopes of a Lancastrian victory had been destroyed at the battle of Barnet in 1471: the Bull of Neville was laid low, and the Sun of York shone triumphant: but the Bull still flourishes, some 200 m down the village street, where a good pub is combined with a high-priced restaurant. Also buried in the abbey was the Earl of Salisbury, one of Edward III's paladins, and a founder member of the Order of the Garter. At the dissolution, the abbey passed to an energetic and influential family called Hoby, though for some years beforehand it was held by Henry VIII for Anne of Cleves; and it is possible that Elizabeth I stayed here as a child. Subsequently, it was owned by the family of Vansittart.

Apart from a few fragments of the Templars' preceptory, the old parts of Bisham Abbey are those built by the Hobys in the sixteenth century. The family can be splendidly seen in the alabaster Hoby monuments in the church of All Saints, at the further end of the village. The two brothers, Sir Philip and Sir Thomas, lie in casual ease: but Sir Thomas's widow Elizabeth, who clearly exercised a dominant influence, is depicted at prayer surrounded by her many children – whether pre-deceased or surviving. And her daughter-in-law Margaret has as her monument a beautiful symbolic obelisk crowned by a heart and guarded by swans. The tower of the church is twelfth-century.

From the Bisham war memorial it is 1 mile along the road to Marlow Bridge (and for those walking in the direction opposite to this text, an alternative routing through Marlow and regaining Stage 8 at Quarry Wood road can be made as described in Stage 8). Marlow has several attractive features: a mini-suspension bridge (of 1836); a large early nineteenth century church (All Saints); Marlow Place in Station Road (1720, Archer); and an unspoilt High Street. And besides, several pubs, hotels, and restaurants of which the most famous is the Compleat Angler which has an incomparable view of the old town and of the Thames tumbling over the weir.

But all this is a prelude to Stage 9 which begins along the small lane from Bisham to Temple Mills, going around Bisham Abbey and then following the right bank of the Thames. Temple Mills, named after the Templar preceptory at Bisham and the water-mill, latterly used for producing paper and previously a brass foundry, is a small cluster of buildings, now being redeveloped. Part of the redevelopment involves houses on the island leading to the weir. After Temple Mills comes a section of paths through woods which, when it reaches the Thames, can be very muddy or even water-logged; in which case short deviations may be necessary and the alternative is to continue along the road described as a surfaced farm road, into Hurley and thence back to the river. Earlier, the path leads under a small road through a remarkable pedestrian tunnel, supported by wooden pillars which appear to have been railway sleepers. Next comes Hurley. Before it, after it and around it are a series of caravan sites and car-access points which seriously detract from the seclusion of the Thames over a length of around $1\frac{1}{4}$ miles: let us hope that in the future restrictions can be imposed. However, amongst them is the Frogmill Camping Site, $\frac{1}{2}$ mile to the west, which can be approached from either Hurley or Frogmill.

Hurley lock is graced with a beautiful island garden and a backdrop of old boat-buildings: a peaceful scene. But in *Our Mutual Friend*, Dickens described a violent fight at 'Flashwater Weir Mill Lock' which evidence suggests was Hurley Lock: 'Bradley was drawing to the lock-edge. Riderhead was drawing away from it. It was a strong grapple and a fierce struggle, arm and leg. Bradley got him round, with his back to the lock, and still worked him backwards.' They both fell in by the lock, and both were drowned.

On recrossing from the island to the right bank, we find a narrow path ahead which leads into Hurley, a deviation inland of 200 m. Here can be seen various remains of another monastery, Hurley Priory. The church of St Mary is the former nave of the Benedictine chapel; and although it is closed (keys obtainable), the Norman doors and windows can be admired from the outside. Between it and the river is a house which was the refectory range. To the west of the church is a round dovecote and a barn, both fourteenth-century. Beyond the church is an open space where formerly stood a Tudor house owned by Lord Lovelace, who here plotted against James II. Macaulay, the historian of that Glorious Revolution, gives it one of his inimitable descriptions: 'His mansion, built by his ancestors out of the spoils of Spanish galleons from the Indies, rose on the ruins of a house of Our Lady in that beautiful valley through which the Thames, not yet defiled by the precincts of a great capital, nor rising and falling with the flow and ebb of the sea, rolls under woods of beech round the gentle hills of Berkshire.' A little further on come village buildings, which contain a shop, post-office, pub (the Rising Sun) and the Old Bell hotel, which bills itself as the oldest inn in England. The whole village is delightful, but it does become very overrun with cars and visitors during summer weekends.

After Hurley and Frogmill, on the farther bank we see Medmenham Abbey, yet another former religious house to justify the quotation for this Stage. And additionally Medmenham was indeed 'condemned to uses vile' when it was in the ownership of the notorious Sir Francis Dashwood. Dashwood had helped to found the Dilettante Society, which Horace Walpole described as 'a club for which the nominal qualification is having been to Italy, and the real one, being drunk'. Geoffrey Knapton painted the leading members in costumes and attitudes that tickled their fancy. Lord Hyde is depicted in somewhat drag clothes; Lord le Despencer is shown as a monk leering at a female statue; Viscount Galway is dressed as a cardinal. In 1745 Dashwood founded 'the Franciscans of Medmenham', also known as the Hell-fire Club, taking as its motto '*Fay ce que vouldras*' from Rabelais' community of monks in *Gargantua*. They indulged in most known forms of depravation, including celebrations of a Black Mass, until the scandal became too great and they dispersed. Of the former Cistercian abbey virtually nothing remains, and what appears from across the river to be such is in fact an eighteenth-century decorative 'ruined' tower. The house is now improbably occupied by RAF Signals' Command. Just upstream from the house is a monument which was put up after a successful legal action in which it was established that the ferry was a public one; but, alas, there is now no ferry, public or private. Medmenham is also the termination of the Chiltern Hundreds, which follow the left bank of the river up from Eton.

After a pleasant stretch of river the route leaves the bank and passes through the estate of Culham Court. It can be a confusing section, but the important thing to realise is that the public footpath which we use passes midway between the big red-brick house and the river. At one point it goes through the garden, where we can see both up and down, and appreciate the skilful juxtaposition of house, garden, river and landscape. Culham Court was built in 1770, and is one of the few large houses on the Walk which is still in private ownership. Beyond it, at Aston, is a hotel called the Flower Pot Inn, which announces that it caters for boating parties, but will certainly

Culham Court

look after walking parties also; drinks and snacks only.

After Aston the farm track leading towards Remenham gives us a good view of the line of the Chilterns curving around the loop of the Thames near Hambleden. We walk along the edge of the Greenlands estate, now owned by the National Trust, and extending into the hills beyond the river. Greenlands House – a large white building surrounded by cedars – can at one point be seen. It was built for W. H. Smith, a Victorian self-made man who rose to be First Lord of the Admiralty – 'I polished those buttons so successfully, that now I am the ruler of the Queen's Navee.' In the Civil War, a former house at Greenlands was a stronghold for the Royalists, until it surrendered to a Parliamentarian force from Henley in June 1644.

In the little hamlet of Remenham we find St Nicholas's church, nineteenth-century but with one medieval window on the north side, and distinguished also by a Norman-style semicircular apse instead of the usual square east end. From here we return to the river, and can see, a little downstream, Temple Island, so named from the decorative cupola atop a cottage designed by James Wyatt. The island is luxuriant with trees, and a willow partly disguises the little 'temple'. A little upstream, and visible along an avenue of poplars on the further bank, lies Fawley Court, a fine eighteenth-century mansion notable for the plasterwork and stucco within.

Henley reach is a straight stretch of river of $1\frac{1}{2}$ miles. It was this unusual feature on the twisting Thames that drew the early rowing enthusiasts here to organise their races. The regular Henley Royal Regatta has been held since 1839, and is the premier regatta in Britain. In late June or early July individuals and teams from schools, colleges and clubs propel themselves up the 1 mile 550 yard course, which is protected from other boats by wooden booms to give an unencumbered width of 80 feet. The eights enter for the Grand Challenge Cup and also for the Ladies' Plate and Princess Elizabeth Cup, which is for schools and colleges; the fours for the Wyfold, Visitors, or Stewards Cups; the pairs for the Silver Goblets; and the scullers for the Diamond Sculls. The fastest recorded time

Temple Island

for the course was 6 minutes 13 seconds (Harvard and also Leander, both in 1975) – around 13 miles per hour. The course starts by Temple Island and ends a few hundred metres short of Henley Bridge. Here are the grandstands and the stewards' enclosure, where sartorial standards are still of importance: but unlike the top-hats and tails of Ascot, the male uniform consists of colourful caps, blazers or boating-jackets, each proclaiming its wearer's rowing prowess – however distant it may now be. Thus an elderly gentleman may be seen in his Leander cap, Oxford blue blazer and Eton Vikings' tie. Just beyond the grandstand is the Leander Club itself, where everything is pink: the club colour, the healthy cheeks of the members, their ties and socks, and often the food they eat – tomato soup, salmon, strawberry ices, etc., perhaps washed down with pink gin or vin rosé. '*Corpus Leandri spes mea*' ('the body of Leander is my hope') is their curiously pagan motto.

And so up to Henley Bridge (1786), graced with allegorical portrait-heads of Thames and Isis, with Henley on the opposite shore promising well-earned comforts and well-appreciated sights.

Tissot: Henley Regatta

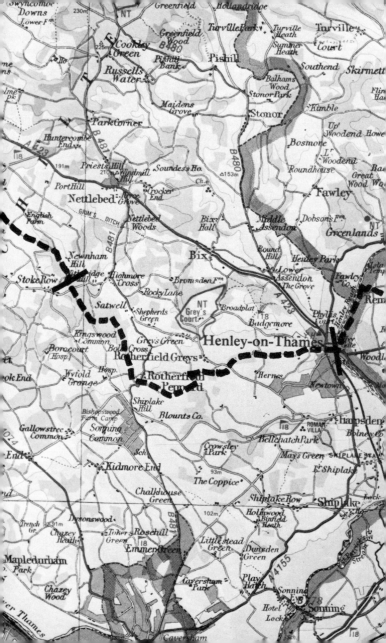

SPECIFICS

This stage leads 120 m uphill from the Thames at Henley into the Chiltern Hills, and is mostly through woods, especially in its second half from Rotherfield Peppard. In all, just over a mile is on streets and lanes, and the rest on earth paths, and across a few fields in the first half.

ROUTE OUTBOUND

From Henley Bridge to the Crooked Billet, Stoke Row 6½ miles (10·5 km)

(a) From Henley Bridge to Rotherfield Peppard Church 3½ miles (6 km)

From Henley bridge go up Hart Street to Market Place and right of the Town Hall up West Street. At the end of West Street, left for a few metres to continue walking uphill up Gravel Hill Road, passing an ornamental lodge gate. 150 m beyond, turn left into Pack and Prime Lane. This soon reduces to a path which leads on for over a mile, initially alongside a wall, then between fields, and then across a farm road and into woods. The route then crosses a public road and leads across a field half right towards a cottage. Here it joins a tarmac lane. A ¼ mile on, this lane turns left at a cross-lanes; 150 m after that, take a signposted footpath right through a wood and on across a field. Then on higher ground at a stile veer half left across two further fields in the general direction of a small church spire. On gaining a lane, follow it rightwards and to Rotherfield Peppard church.

(b) From Rotherfield Peppard Church to the Crooked Billet, Stoke Row 3 miles (4·5 km)

From Rotherfield Peppard church, go along Church Lane to Rotherfield Peppard green. Walk on to the green and keep close to

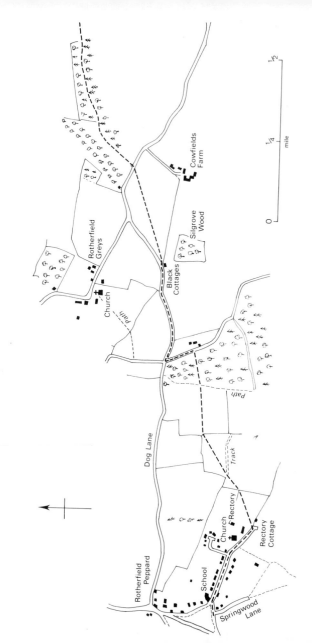

Rotherfield Peppard

Dog Lane

Rotherfield Greys

Church

Path

Black Cottages

Silgrove Wood

Cowfields Farm

School

Church

Rectory

Track

Path

Rectory Cottage

Springwood Lane

0   ¼   ½
         mile

the left-hand edge of it. Cross the B481 road on to a lane with a weight-limit notice. Follow it for $\frac{1}{4}$ mile, then, where it turns left at the bottom of a hill, go straight ahead on to a bridleway which continues along the base of the valley for 1 mile. During the course of this mile it enters a beech-wood and two paths leading up to the left must be rejected, as well as what appears to be the main track of the bridleway which inclines slowly up to the right, where our true path keeps to the base of the valley. The point at which our route leads up at right angles to the left is halfway along a section of the beech-wood where to our left a clearing separates the woods (though this clearing may in time become reafforested). If you come to a cottage while still continuing along the base of the valley, you have gone $\frac{1}{4}$ mile too far. Take the bridleway up to the left as described: it leads through the Forestry Commission's plantation of Greyhone Wood. At the end of this, at a point where several paths meet, a plaque announces another plantation – Burnt Platt Wood. Enter this and immediately take a path leading obliquely up and to the right along the edge of it. $\frac{1}{4}$ mile on, pass through a gate out of the plantation and continue in the same direction as before along the outer edge, and under deciduous trees. Where the path comes alongside an earth bank, fork right a few metres further on, and pass by and close to the left of a rough plantation. The path then leads on downhill to cross a road just by a house (Clare Cottage). Go across this road on to another signposted path which leads up along the upper edge of a beech-wood until it meets a small road. Then walk straight ahead to the Crooked Billet public house.

ROUTE INBOUND

From the Crooked Billet, Stoke Row, to Henley Bridge 6$\frac{1}{2}$ miles (10·5 km)

(a) From the Crooked Billet, Stoke Row, to Rotherfield Peppard Church 3 miles (4·5 km)
Emerging from the Crooked Billet public house, take the lane leading left. 200 m on, where this lane turns right, leave it and keep straight ahead along the upper edge of a beech-wood. The path

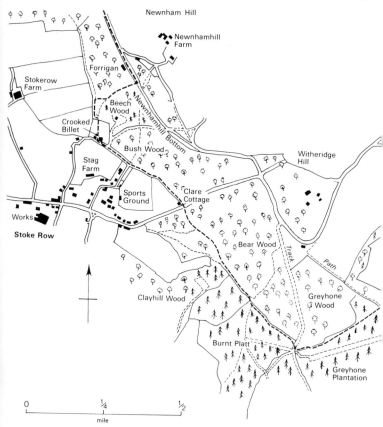

leads downwards and crosses a road just by a house (Clare Cottage).
Then, by a signposted footpath go ahead and uphill, afterwards
keeping close to the right of a rough plantation of conifers. The path
then leads down and up and passes close to an earth bank and then
alongside a Forestry Commission plantation on the right. Where
there is a gate into this plantation (Burnt Platt Wood), go through
the gate and then turn left along a ride, continuing, now inside the

plantation, in the same direction as before. The ride leads
downwards to where several paths meet. Enter Greyhone Wood,
another Forestry Commission plantation, at a plaque and follow a
signposted bridleway. This bridleway leads straight and
progressively downhill, leaving Greyhone Wood and crossing an
unforested – or newly forested – gap before arriving at a beech-
wood at the bottom of a valley. Here turn right and continue along
the bridleway, keeping always to the bottom of the valley, for
1 mile. Where it comes to a tarmac lane, take this lane leftwards and
uphill but keeping right at a fork soon after. The lane leads to
Rotherfield Peppard green. From here, cross the B481 road and
walk across the green into Church Lane and up to the church.

(b) From Rotherfield Peppard Church to Henley Bridge 3½ miles
(6 km)
Leaving from the church gate, follow around to the left along a lane.
100 m on, at a double footpath sign, take the path half left
diagonally across two fields, down and up, and then slightly right
across a third field directly towards and then through a wood. At a
tarmac lane turn left for 150 m, then follow the lane sharp right. On
for ¼ mile as far as a cottage on the right, where there is a sign for two
footpaths: take the left-hand path which leads diagonally across a
field to a road. Cross the road and enter a signposted bridleway
which leads on for 1½ miles, originally through a wood and then,
after crossing a farm track, through fields; finally skirting a wall.
This bridleway (Pack and Prime Lane) emerges on to a road (Gravel
Hill). Here turn right downhill. 150 m on, after passing an
ornamental lodge, go left and then immediately right, to enter West
Street, a small street parallel to Gravel Hill. Follow West Street
down through Market Place to Hart Street and on to Henley Bridge.

APPROACH BY CAR

Approach Henley-on-Thames is in Oxfordshire, 8 miles north of
Reading, at the junction of the A423 and A4155. Rotherfield
Peppard is on the B481, halfway between Reading and Nettlebed.
Stoke Row is approached off the B481, or off the A4074 between

Reading and Wallingford.   **Parking** Henley: car park off Market Place. Rotherfield Peppard: park at church. Stoke Row: park on side roads; Crooked Billet is in Newland Lane.   **Taxis** Henley Taxis (tel. 4937).

APPROACH BY PUBLIC TRANSPORT

Trains British Rail Station at Henley ($\frac{1}{4}$ mile from Henley bridge). **Buses** Oxford South Midland at Henley (Hart Street/New Street); and Alder Valley at Stoke Row (to Reading every 2 hours, not on Sundays, $\frac{1}{2}$ hour journey time).

PUBLIC TRANSPORT FROM END OF STAGE 10

To start of Stages 10, 9, 8 and 7 No convenient public transport. Nearest is Oxford South Midland at Nettlebed, 2 miles from Stoke Row (every 2 hours: journey time to Henley 12 minutes and to Maidenhead 36 minutes).

ACCOMMODATION

Hotels Henley: the Red Lion (tel. 2161).   **Guest houses and small hotels** Henley: see Stage 9.   **Youth hostel** See Stage 9.   **Camping** Henley, Swiss Farm (tel. 3205) – open March–October. Stoke Row: Crooked Billet (by permission).

REFRESHMENT

Restaurants and snacks A choice at Henley.   **Pubs** The Old White Hart, Henley; the Dog, Rotherfield Peppard; the Crooked Billet, Stoke Row.

TIMES OF ADMISSION

Houses and Museums Greys Court: April–September 14.15–18.00, gardens weekdays and house Monday, Wednesday and Friday; closed Good Friday.

FACILITIES

Telephone Rotherfield Peppard green.

DESCRIPTION

In mud and elder-scented shade
A reach away the breach is made
    By dive and shout
    That circles out
To Henley tower and town;
And 'Boats for Hire' the rafters ring,
And pink on white the roses cling
And red the bright geraniums swing
In baskets hanging down.

John Betjeman, 1906–
from 'Henley-on-Thames'

Appropriately, the first two buildings on either side of the road at
the entry into Henley from the bridge are both eighteenth-century
inns – the Angel and the Red Lion. For Henley was a staging-point,
a half-way halt between London and Oxford on one of the two main
roads between the two cities (the other via High Wycombe). Here
many famous travellers spent the night, and the Red Lion
appropriately recalls them in the names of its bedrooms, amongst
which are the Charles I room, the General Blücher room, the Duke
of Marlborough room, Dr Johnson's room, and the Prince Regent's
room. There is also Prince Rupert's room, which recalls that Henley
was a border town in the Civil War, and suffered a lot from the
garrisoning of troops and the expressions of hatred that soured the
inhabitants. The Red Lion is still the best accommodation in
Henley, and beyond Henley there is none on our route before
Wallingford, 14 miles on. At the bridge also we can see a series of
boathouses which cater for pleasure-craft and rowing-boats:
formerly, these wharves would have been busy with trade, for
Henley was also an important river-port and the commercial centre

Siberechts: Landscape with Rainbow, Henley-on-Thames

for a wide area of the Chilterns.

Beyond the inns the vista into Hart Street is partly blocked by the chequer-pattern walls of St Mary's church, surmounted by its fine sixteenth-century tower, made taller by four battlemented pinnacles, dominating the town and river. The spacious interior gives a light and pleasing effect, and comprises several periods of construction from the fourteenth century onwards. It contains a fine seventeenth-century monument to Dame Elizabeth Periam, a local benefactor who founded a school here. There is also a memorial to General Dumouriez, the victor of Valmy and Foreign Minister of revolutionary France. He fled from Napoleon in 1804 and took refuge near Henley, where he lived for many years until his death in 1823. The churchyard should not be missed: it is bordered by two rows of old (though rebuilt) almshouses and by the Chantry House, a wooden-framed structure of around 1400.

Hart Street is a busy shopping centre and includes several tearooms, which can be very welcome after a long day's walk. It contains a few sixteenth-century buildings, including the Old White Hart Inn, and a group opposite the church in one of which lived William Lenthall, who was Speaker of the House of Commons on the occasion when Charles I entered the chamber and personally arrested five members. There are also several houses of the Georgian period. Hart Street becomes progressively broader up the hill towards the Market Place and Town Hall.

After the miniature charm of West Street and the architectural joke in the flamboyant lodge to Friar Park, we leave Henley as suddenly as we entered it, a warm and colourful interlude in our green walk and a worthy introduction into the county of Oxfordshire in which we now remain to the end of the Walk. Incidentally, Henley is the starting-point of the Oxfordshire Way, a long-distance path that leads across the county to Bourton-on-the-Water, and which joins our Walk again at our extremity in Extension B: 5 miles out from Henley it passes close by Stonor Park, a great house too far off course to be included here as a diversion from our route.

In Pack and Prime Lane we become aware of the undulating ground and generally upward slope; for it is here that we enter the Chilterns, which lead us in this Stage from a start at a height of

32 m to an end at 155 m. At the same time we also become aware of the chalk from which the Chilterns are made. The progression of history and the development of architecture appear as brilliant but almost instantaneous flashes when set against the aeons of pre-history and geology. A million years into the past, like a light-year into space, is hard to comprehend. Yet if anyone can do so, a long-distance walker traversing a geological feature stands a better chance than most as he slowly plods across the land. In Stages 10 and 11 we are walking on a bed of chalk some 250 m thick. It consists of incalculable millions of marine organisms – mostly planktonic algae – which disintegrated to form a sediment at the bottom of the sub-tropical seas which covered the land during the Cretaceous period 136–65 million years ago. It took about 25 million years to form this chalk bed, at the rate of about one inch for each 2,500 years. When the sea retreated, the surface of the chalk was flat. But then during several ice-ages, of which the most recent lasted till around 70,000 years ago, the force of the superimposed glaciers and the waters which emanated from the glaciers moulded the chalk beds into the hills and downs as we now see them, and ground down exposed rocks to gravel, to drift downhill and mix with clays in the valleys.

Pack and Prime Lane leads us between elder-hedges and then through beeches to cross a road and thence to a field and lane towards Rotherfield Peppard. But before we get there, at the point in the route described as where the lane turns sharply left, a diversion of half a mile would take us to Rotherfield Greys. This diversion can be made by taking a signposted bridleway to the right for 200 m, then right again on to a footpath across fields to the village. Rotherfield Greys Church is virtually all nineteenth-century, but its great glory is the Knollys monument, an immense seventeenth-century memorial to Sir Francis Knollys, who was first cousin and High Treasurer to Elizabeth I, and his family. Made of marble and alabaster their effigies lie or kneel under an elaborate canopy full of decorative devices. The church also contains a very fine brass monument to Lord Robert de Grey, who died in 1387. Three-quarters of a mile beyond Rotherfield Greys Church lies Greys Court (now owned by the National Trust) where first the de Greys and then the Knollyses held sway. It is essentially a fortified manor-

house, with a tower and lots of walls between which a beautiful garden has been created, cleverly designed to give a series of separate and distinct visual effects.

The route approaches Rotherfield Peppard from across fields, in which appropriately there may be cattle, since 'rother' is Old English for 'cattle'. All Saints' Church was really completely rebuilt in 1874; but this comparatively recent achievement is also a very successful one, with the interior well-proportioned and convincing, well lit from the south and with a sloping-roofed aisle to the north. Remnants of a Norman church exist in the chancel arch and windows. The reredos is made of a beautifully executed wood engraving of the Last Supper, after Leonardo da Vinci. The exterior is flint-covered, and the spire, clock and lych-gate complete the picture of a well-accoutred English parish church.

A little further on, the village is distinguished by its triangular green, around which houses are grouped on two sides: it is unfortunately marred by a main road through the middle. The common land extends westwards, to where we descend into a small valley. These village commons used to be far more extensive, and although those that remain are seldom used for their original purpose, which was the grazing of sheep and cattle, their existence is a pleasing change from the near-universality of private or corporate ownership.

After this we enjoy a 2½ mile stretch through woods to the end of the Stage. A special feature of the Chilterns, unlike their chalky equivalents in Berkshire or in Sussex, is that they are one of the most wooded areas of England: and not only by plantation, but by natural growth. Although in prehistoric times oak and ash predominated, beech is now more common: and these great trees still give me the most satisfaction when in large groves and woods, in which their size and smooth grey barks are all the more impressive for the lack of undergrowth which they have so effectively overshadowed. On our route on this section through Great Bottom Wood and then Oveys Wood they look even larger than usual because they reach up the valley on either side of us. The Forestry Commission's fir-plantations give a different impression: serried

Rotherfield Peppard church

ranks of timber planted in 1960–2, red cedar (Thuja) and hemlock in Greyhone Wood and pine in Burnt Platt Wood. Then we revert to deciduous trees in Bear Wood. A little to our right, but invisible through the trees, is Witheridge Hill, an outlying patch of gravel and clay and thus different geologically from the rest of Stages 10 and 11.

This last section through the woods can be confusing, and it may be that the road up towards Stoke Row will be gained at a spot higher or lower than intended. If so, the aim should be to walk up or down it until you find Clare Cottage, which stands by itself on the other side of the road, at the upper end of a section of wood. The Crooked Billet public house is the termination of Stage 10: but for those wishing to enter Stoke Row village, it will be better to leave the route by the road into Stoke Row which we cross by Clare Cottage. Within ½ mile leftwards will be found in the village two other pubs, a post office, a village shop and an occasional bus service to Reading: also the Maharajah's Well, the now disused gift of an Indian potentate.

SPECIFICS

This Stage first goes up 50 m to the ridge of the Chilterns and then, with good views of the Oxfordshire plain ahead, descends 160 m to join the Thames near Wallingford. For nearly 2 miles it makes use of an ancient raised earthwork known as Grim's Ditch, which can be very muddy at its lower end, but otherwise the route is firm and mostly on farm tracks and drives. Somewhat over half a mile is on public lanes: nearly 2 miles are through woods.

ROUTE OUTBOUND

From the Crooked Billet, Stoke Row, to Wallingford Bridge 7 miles (11·5 km) See map on p. 176

Immediately past the Crooked Billet public house (right as you leave the front door) take a signposted footpath right into an orchard and field and downhill to a hedge. The path then enters a paddock, leaves it briefly through a copse, then re-enters it. The path then crosses the paddock in a downhill direction, leaving it finally through a kissing gate adjoining a farm gate. Thence downhill through a wood to reach a tarmac lane at the bottom of a valley. Here turn left, past several houses, the first 'Forrigan'. Where a sign for a house marked 'Syde' is seen, follow the tarmac lane as it turns left upwards and into the beech-wood. It ends at the last of the houses. Our route continues as a bridleway which initially is a narrow path between hedges soon leaving the wood, then becoming a farm track, and then, after Whitcalls Farm, a tarmac drive. It then continues across a road and on, always in the same direction, ignoring footpath signs to the left and right, passing to the left of, and a field away from, Upper House Farm, to reach the ridge of the Chilterns at 202 m. Still in the same direction, the right of way comes alongside and then enters Mongewell Woods at a point where it passes a green wooden hut. Soon after this, reject one path to the

left and soon after reject one to the right, keeping generally
downhill. Where Mongewell Woods end, go on down between fields
and then past a wood, and past Woodhouse Farm. At a public road,
turn right for 400 m. Then go left into a raised path (Grim's Ditch).
This soon traverses a road diagonally, and then leads downwards to
the A4074 road. Cross this road and continue straight ahead at a
sign for 'Ridgeway' and through a belt of wood alongside Carmel
College driveway. After crossing a college drive, continue still in the
wood to where a paved path crosses. Here turn right, and continue
along a bridleway and to the left of a modern college building. At
Newnham Farm continue in the same direction between farm
buildings, going to the left of brick cottages at a footpath sign. 50 m
after a farm gate, turn left for 150 m to reach the Thames, then right
and up the towpath to Wallingford bridge. Go under the bridge and
mount by stone stairs to the bridge, to cross the Thames.

ROUTE INBOUND

From Wallingford Bridge to the Crooked Billet, Stoke Row 7 miles
(11·5 km) See map on p. 176

At Wallingford bridge cross to the left bank of the Thames,
descending on the upstream side of the bridge by stone stairs. Walk
under the bridge and downstream along the river bank for under
$\frac{1}{2}$ mile; then at a footpath sign turn left and away from the river for
150 m, then right and through a gate between farm buildings.
Continue straight ahead along a bridleway past a modern college
building on the left. Then, just after joining paving, turn left into a
belt of wood at a sign for the Ridgeway. Follow up through the
wood along an ill-defined path, crossing a college drive at one point,
up to the A4074 road. Cross this and continue uphill along the
raised bank of Grim's Ditch. Eventually this traverses a road
diagonally: soon afterwards, where it crosses a second road, leave
Grim's Ditch and turn right along the road for 400 m. Then turn left
up the tarmac drive leading to Woodhouse Farm. After the farm,
the road becomes unpaved. It soon leaves the wood which is on the
right, to go uphill and between fields and thence into Mongewell

woods. It continues uphill through the woods, always in the same
general direction. After passing a green wooden hut, it emerges from
the wood; and then, soon after houses on the left, it reaches the
ridge of the Chilterns at 202 m. Thence on along a driveway,
eventually tarmac, and rejecting footpath signs to left and right.
Across a public road and straight ahead along another tarmac
driveway to Whitcalls Farm. After this farm the road degenerates
into a farm track and then into a path before gaining a paved road
in a beech-wood. This road then passes by several houses in, and
later beside, the wood. Just after a house called 'Forrigan' on the
right, and a wooden structure in a field on the left, a footpath sign
can be seen by a gate into the wood on the right. Take this path up
through woods to a paddock. The right of way then leads ahead
across the paddock, then up and to the left, through some trees, into
the paddock again, and thence through a hedge and across a stile
into a field and orchard and up to the Crooked Billet public house.

APPROACH BY CAR

Approach Stoke Row is a village in South Oxfordshire, approached
off the A4074 between Reading and Wallingford, or the B481
between Reading and Nettlebed. Wallingford is 12 miles south of
Oxford, accessible from several A roads, including the A423.
Parking At Stoke Row, in side streets: the Crooked Billet is in
Newland Lane. In Wallingford, St Alban's car park by Market
Place.   **Taxis** Wallingford: Hill's Taxis (tel. 37022) or Frank's Taxis
(tel. 37163).

APPROACH BY PUBLIC TRANSPORT

Trains (British Rail station at Didcot, 6 miles from Wallingford).
Buses Oxford South Midland at Wallingford (Market Place); and
Stoke Row (to Reading, every 2 hours, not on Sundays: journey
time $\frac{1}{2}$ hour).

PUBLIC TRANSPORT FROM END OF STAGE 11

To start of Stage 11 No convenient public transport. Nearest is Oxford South Midland bus from Wallingford to Nettlebed, 2 miles from Stoke Row. **To start of Stages 10 and 8** Oxford South Midland buses from Wallingford to Henley and Maidenhead respectively (every 2 hours, journey time 30 and 50 minutes respectively). **To start of Stage 9** As for Stage 8, then Alder Valley bus to Marlow (hourly, journey time 25 minutes).

ACCOMMODATION

Hotel The George Hotel, Wallingford (tel. 36665). **Guest houses and small hotels** Winterbrook Lodge, Wallingford (tel. 37151). **Camping** Riverside Park, Wallingford (tel. 36969) – open Easter– September. Crooked Billet, Stoke Row (by permission).

REFRESHMENT

Restaurants and snacks At Wallingford. **Pubs** The Crooked Billet, Stoke Row; the Town Arms, Wallingford.

FACILITIES

Tourist information Wallingford (tel. 36969).

DESCRIPTION

Before the Roman came to Rye or out of Severn strode,
The rolling English drunkard made the rolling English road.
A reeling road, a rolling road, that rambles round the shire,
And after him the parson ran, the sexton and the squire;
A merry road, a mazy road, and such as we did tread
The night we went to Birmingham by way of Beachy Head.

G. K. Chesterton, 1874–1936
from 'The Rolling English Road'

The Crooked Billet public house at Stoke Row is distinguished by
the unusual feature of having no bar. The landlord brings you your
drink from a cavernous area at the back, while you sit in a
comfortable room at the front which has an enormous fireplace, and
usually a blazing open fire during winter weekends. This is how all
inns would have been until bars were progressively introduced
within the last hundred years, and now it adds a special sense of
occasion to take a drink in such a setting, even though the Crooked
Billet is only a very small pub and provides only the simplest snacks.

  Stage 11 starts with a $\frac{1}{4}$ mile of twisting footpath downhill,
skirting around and then through a paddock on what is obviously a
deviation from its original course. The next section is along a small
paved access road to some modern houses in Bush Wood. Somehow
they look out of place, these smart residences set within the beech-
grove: one feels they should have been placed at the edge of the
wood rather than dotted about within it. After this we emerge into
farmland. Up here on the top of the Chilterns it is mixed farming,
arable land and pasturage for cattle and at present, evidently, for
pigs rather than sheep. At a point near Upper House Farm we reach
the watershed of the Chilterns at 202 m (our highest point in the

The Crooked Billet

entire Walk), and obtain our first view of the Oxfordshire plain. Then comes ¾ mile through woods, here mostly of small growth. These, like other woods in the area, are shot over in the autumn; and in them we may see pheasants, besides other birds such as woodcock or jays. The jays, proclaiming their presence with a frightful shriek, are the easiest to hear. The pheasants, strutting around and reluctant to fly, are the easiest to observe.

At the lower edge of Mongewell Woods we get our second view of the plain ahead: but this time it is slightly scarred by the distant cooling-towers of the Didcot power station, with their plumes of white smoke. Although the Walk later closes to within 3 miles of them, they are almost continually obscured by intervening features; and it is only from this distant prospect that they cast a pall of industrial doom over the otherwise rustic landscape. From here our route descends through another farm, and actually between the farm buildings and a house which satisfies all one's most idyllic notions of what a farmhouse should be like.

In the 3¾ miles since Bush Wood we have been walking along a mostly unpaved road, such as would have passed for a main road in former centuries, and which gives us an idea of what walking would have been like in the past – not so much a question of footpaths, as of a steady tramp along a traffic-free 'hard-high-road'. And although no Englishman, drunk or sober, could have made any road before the Roman came (because the English only arrived in the island in the fourth century), this section also provides for us a mild but distinctive roll, that inconsequential twist that so distinguishes roads made for men from roads made for cars.

But at the end of Woodhouse Farm, where we turn right for a mere 400 m, we are on a really significant road of ancient times – the Icknield Way. This is the oldest prehistoric track in England, and parts of it date from as far back as 1800 BC. It leads from Avebury in Wiltshire into East Anglia, following the lines of the hills and avoiding as far as possible the low-lying areas, then so hazardous with marsh and undergrowth of thorn and bramble and wild beasts. The people who first formed the Icknield Way were of the later Stone Age period: a people of Mediterranean origin who came here

Grim's Ditch leading towards the Chilterns

from Iberia. At that time a primitive form of agriculture and animal husbandry was developing, and the Icknield Way, which was more a series of interweaving tracks than a single way (except at fords and other difficult features), would have been used as a great drove road along which herds were driven.

We know very little about these prehistoric people, and though at times they may have lived in social tranquillity, at others they probably had to endure most appalling suffering, whether from nature or man. Of one thing we may be sure: they were of necessity great long-distance walkers, and infinitely more skilled than modern man in following the track and sensing the direction. On this Stage, their flint implements – for digging and cutting – have been uncovered at Blenheim Farm (close to where we join Grim's Ditch) and at Mongewell (near where we leave it). And at Mongewell also have been found their stone bowls – for keeping food or liquids. Nor should we forget primitive man, who had lived in the Thames Valley area for hundreds of thousands of years before, even before the last ice age, amid quite different vegetation and in a climate and surroundings that at times would have resembled the tropical forests of Brazil and at others, the tundra of Northern Canada. Because of this very different environment it is far harder for us to imagine his savage life, though he too walked through the land, hunting and foraging.

The short section of the Icknield Way which permits these reflections leads northwards along the road and 2 miles on comes to Ewelme, perhaps the most exquisite of all Chiltern villages, with a cluster of fifteenth-century buildings – almshouses and school and a church that miraculously was spared the attentions of the puritan iconoclasts.

Grim's Ditch, the feature along which we next walk for $1\frac{3}{4}$ miles, is of an altogether later date than the Icknield Way. It is of English sixth-century origin: though whether it was a national boundary (between Mercia and Wessex) or a more local one is open to dispute. Grim was another name for Woden or Wotan, the chief nordic god, and merely denotes the awe with which subsequent generations viewed these ancient earthworks. Woden, incidentally,

Wallingford from across the Thames

was a wanderer, given to appearing incognito dressed in a long dark-blue mantle and brown broad-brimmed hat; and as such would be in sympathy with long-distance walkers – '*Wandrer heist mich die Welt; weit wandert' ich schon: auf der Erde Rükken rüht' ich mich weil.*' Walking along the top of Grim's Ditch gives us some excellent views on either hand, even though we are pleasantly enclosed by hawthorn, elder, bramble and gorse. For the full length of our walk along it we are on a section of the Ridgeway Path, an official national long-distance path of 85 miles, which follows broadly along the line of the Icknield Way from Avebury in Wiltshire to Ivinghoe in Buckinghamshire. After the A4074 the raised embankment disappears, and the path is much more like the ditch its name denotes. Here it can be very muddy, since also it is apparently extensively used by equestrians.

Mongewell Park is now a school, called Carmel College; and on leaving Grim's Ditch we pass by a new college building. From here we come to the small church of St Mary, Newnham Murren (closed): externally, most of what we see, including the narrow lancet window, is of the restoration of 1849 but the doorway on the north side is Norman (eleventh-century), as is also the chancel arch within. Then, after passing through Newnham Farm, we rejoin the Thames and see on the further bank the town of Wallingford, with its eighteenth-century houses with gardens backing on to the river, and the unusual spire of St Peter's church: and so up towards Wallingford Bridge, which has five arches spanning the Thames and a further twelve across the low ground beside the river. It is mostly of eighteenth-century construction, although three of the arches on the upstream side are medieval, and can be distinguished by their pointed apexes.

Towns and villages, like actors, have their 'exits and their entrances', and nowhere on the Walk is there a better entrance than into Wallingford, proceeding from farmland pasturage across the river into an old main street with things looking much the same as they would have looked two hundred years ago; a clear-cut distinction between country and town very satisfactory to the pedestrian, especially to one who has just walked across the Chilterns.

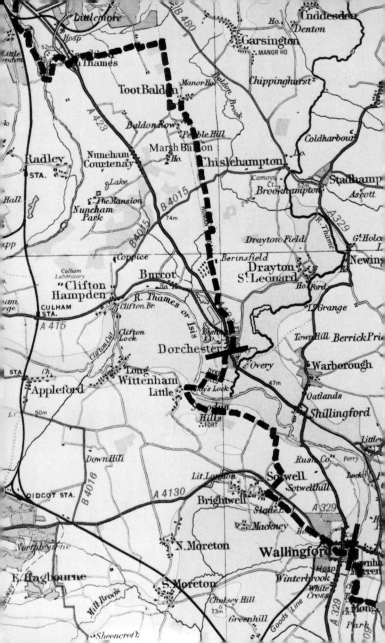

SPECIFICS

The route leaves the Thames at Wallingford and rejoins it just before the end of the Stage, near Dorchester. Apart from one mile in the streets of these historic towns and at Sotwell, it leads on paths and tracks through a nice mixture of arable land, orchard, wood and pasture; and it skirts around the Sinodun Hills, surmounted by the traces of prehistoric fortifications.

ROUTE OUTBOUND

From Wallingford Bridge to Dorchester Abbey 6 miles (9·5 km)

From Wallingford bridge enter Wallingford High Street. Turn left at St Mary's Street (pedestrians only) into Market Place. By the church, turn right into Church Lane and then ahead into Kinecroft. Cross the green diagonally to the right, regaining the road at the junction of the High Street, Croft Road and Station Road. Take Station Road ahead for nearly half a mile. Where Fir Tree Avenue joins Station Road, and just opposite a hospital, take a signposted footpath leading slightly left past houses and then through fields to Sotwell. Here take the village lane which leads on in the same direction. Opposite Brightwell Free Church and post-box, turn right up a narrow path which soon becomes a track. Cross the A4130 road and continue on a waymarked bridleway (tarmac initially) through orchards. At a T junction, turn left uphill to a barn by another T Junction, where turn right, still between orchards. The bridleway leads downhill, twisting left and right as it goes, and joins a farm lane at the base of the hill. Here turn left, through North Farm, and on for $\frac{1}{2}$ mile more to some ruined structures. Then on in the same direction by a path along the edge of a field. Into Little Wittenham wood along a broad ride flanked by cypress trees. At the end, enter a meadow and contour round on it to Little Wittenham church. Here a lane leads down to the Thames, which cross by footbridge. Then immediately go diagonally left across a field and through a gate leading to a path which goes through and then to the right alongside ancient earthworks. Follow this path to its extremity to enter Dorchester by Wittenham Lane. Into Bridge End, past the Roman Catholic church and across the A423 road to Dorchester Abbey.

ROUTE INBOUND

From Dorchester Abbey to Wallingford Bridge 6 miles (9·5 km)

Leaving Dorchester Abbey by the gate to the south of the churchyard cross the A423 road and then bear right to enter Bridge End. Then go into Wittenham Lane and thence onto a footpath which leads along the side of, and later through, ancient earthworks. Where the path reaches a field, a lock can be seen. Head across the field to the left of the lock, and cross the Thames by a footbridge. Past Little Wittenham Church and then to the left by a signposted bridleway contouring across a meadow to enter Little Wittenham wood. Follow bridleway sign at the entrance to the wood, which leads along a broad ride, lined by cypress trees. Then on by a path leading in the same direction at the edge of a field, which soon leads to a lane. Follow this lane to North Farm and on for 200 m, then strike up right at a bridleway path between hedges. On gaining higher ground this path leads between orchards. At a barn, turn left and downhill; then, at a junction in the orchard $\frac{1}{4}$ mile on, turn right along a track, now tarmac. Across the A4130 road and on along a track, then ahead into a narrow pathway. At Sotwell village lane, by the Brightwell Free Church, turn left. Later, where the lane turns left, go straight ahead between two houses ('The Lodge' and 'The Cottage') and thence between fields by a footpath. This path joins Station Road at Fir Tree Avenue. Continue along to the end of Station Road. Here, at the junction of Station Road, Croft Road and the High Street, turn on to a paved path across a green (Kinecroft), and then between houses by the Coach and Horses public house. On into Church Lane and thence to Market Place. Traverse Market Place to the far corner to St Mary's Street

(pedestrians only). Then right into the High Street and down to
Wallingford bridge.

APPROACH BY CAR

Approach Wallingford and Dorchester-on-Thames are both in
Oxfordshire, respectively 12 miles and 8 miles south of Oxford on
the A423. **Parking** Wallingford: St Alban's car park, by Market
Place. Dorchester: Bridge End, opposite the abbey. **Taxis**
Wallingford: Hill's Taxis (tel. 37022). Didcot: Harold's Cars
(tel. 814321).

APPROACH BY PUBLIC TRANSPORT

Trains (British Rail station at Didcot 6 miles from Wallingford and
7 miles from Dorchester). **Buses** Oxford South Midland at
Wallingford (Market Place) and Dorchester (War Memorial).

PUBLIC TRANSPORT FROM END OF STAGE 12

To start of Stage 12 Oxford South Midland bus from Dorchester to
Wallingford (every 2 hours, journey time 12 minutes). **To start of
Stage 11** No convenient public transport. Nearest is Oxford South
Midland bus from Dorchester to Nettlebed, 2 miles from Stoke Row
(every 2 hours, journey time 27 minutes). **To start of Stage 10**
Oxford South Midland bus from Dorchester to Henley (every
2 hours, journey time 40 minutes). **To start of Stage 9** Same as
above, then Alder Valley bus from Henley to Marlow (hourly,
journey time 25 minutes).

ACCOMMODATION

Hotels The George Hotel, Wallingford (tel. 36665). The Shillingford
Bridge Hotel (Warborough 8567). The White Hart Hotel,

Dorchester (Oxford 340074). **Guest houses and small hotels**
Winterbook Lodge, Wallingford (tel. 37151). **Camping** Riverside
Park, Wallingford (tel. 36969) – open Easter–September.

REFRESHMENT

Restaurant Dorchester: the George Hotel. **Pubs** Coach and
Horses, Kinecroft, Wallingford; the Bell, Sotwell; the Fleur de Lys,
Dorchester.

FACILITIES

Tourist Information Wallingford (tel. 36969). **Telephones** Sotwell
and Wittenham. **Toilets** Wallingford Market Place and Dorchester
Bridge End.

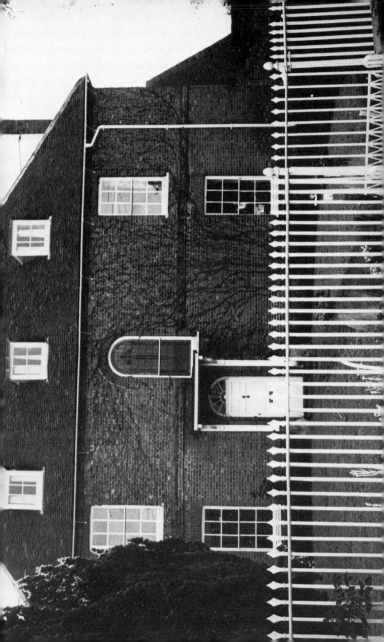

DESCRIPTION

And see you, after rain, the trace
Of mound and ditch and wall?
O that was a Legion's camping-place,
When Caesar sailed for Gaul.
And see you marks that show and fade,
Like shadows on the Downs?
O they are the lines the Flint Men made,
To guard their wondrous towns.
Trackway and Camp and City lost,
Salt marsh where now is corn –
Old Wars, old Peace, old Arts that cease,
And so was England born!

Rudyard Kipling (1865–1936),
from *Puck of Pook's Hill*

Wallingford is now only a small market town, but once it was one of
the most important towns in England. It is probable that the
original Saxon bridge here was the first across the Thames at any
point. After his victory at Hastings William I came by way of
Wallingford in his approach towards London: and at that time it
was certainly the largest town in Berkshire, in which county it was
until 1972. Hence it is not surprising that it became a main strong-
point for the forces of the Empress Matilda and was held by them
against Stephen for twelve years, until relieved by her son Henry II
in 1153, who rewarded the town with a special charter of privileges.
But Wallingford never recovered from the ravages of the Black
Death in the fourteenth century, and afterwards declined in favour
of nearby Abingdon whose powerful Benedictine abbey
progressively outsmarted the smaller priory at Wallingford. Later, in
the Civil War, it was a Royalist stronghold, and the last to surrender
to the Parliamentarians in July 1646, for which defiance Cromwell

Slade End Farm House, Sotwell

ordered its fortifications to be destroyed (or 'slighted'): and so thoroughly was this done that hardly any masonry remains in the castle mound in the north-east corner of the town.

In the nineteenth century it only rated a small railway branch line, and it sank into peaceful repose. But we may now feel thankful that history has thus passed Wallingford by, as we enter the narrow High Street and see a sequence of old houses, including Callova House – a fine eighteenth-century house of red and blue brick – and the seventeenth-century George Hotel, with overhanging gables. Market Place is dominated by the Town Hall (1670) with an open loggia on the ground floor, and behind it is St Mary's Church (1854). On the east side of Market Place stands the old Corn Exchange, recently converted into a theatre.

After this the route proceeds by way of passages to the town green, which marks the western edge of the medieval town, and then along an extension of the High Street that is of little merit. A footpath leads us into the village of Sotwell. Just beyond the Brightwell Free Church (where we turn right) is the nineteenth-century church of St James, Sotwell, with pretty timber-framed black and white cottages around it. In the fields just to the south of us here is Mackney Court Farm, which was selected as a model English farm for Chairman Hua of China to visit in 1979. Next we have $\frac{3}{4}$ mile of orchard. The neat rows of apple trees provide a welcome change from the more usual farm fields.

At the bottom of the hill we come in sight of the Thames. On the further bank is the village of Shillingford, with a lane leading down to the river. The large house on the water's edge, looking very attractive from a distance, is Riverside Court, built in the early twentieth-century for a prosperous tailor. On our side, $\frac{1}{2}$ mile right along the farm road we have just joined is Shillingford bridge (eighteenth-century), with the hotel beside it. Shortly after passing North Farm we cross the line of the Roman road which we shall be walking along in Stage 13: at this point it is heading down to the river at a place known as Old Street Ford. Our route then leads through Little Wittenham Wood, half a mile along a straight woodland ride lined by cypresses, and thence across a meadow to the hamlet of Little Wittenham.

Wittenham Clump

This is the nearest we get to the twin hillocks, 120 m high, known as the Sinodun Hills, or Berkshire Bubs. They can be better seen from points nearer Dorchester or beyond in Stage 13; but to appreciate them properly a short deviation of under $\frac{1}{2}$ mile up the hill at this point will lead us to the top of them. From here their strategic importance can on a clear day be easily understood. For they stand by themselves in a commanding position, dominating the Thames at a point where it approaches the Goring Gap to the south, and leaves its upper valley; and they also lie close to the conjunction of the Berkshire Downs to the west and the Chilterns to the east. It is no exaggeration to say that they represent, geographically, the strategic centre of southern England. Because of this they have been held as a strong-point probably since Stone Age times; and certainly by the time of the Celtic settlements of around 500 BC. This was an important place, and held by either the Atrebates, who occupied land to the south of the Thames, or the Catuvellauni, to the north. On the summit of Castle Hill is a ten-acre earthwork enclosure with an entrance-gap on the west side, and a ditch within, the 'trace of mound and ditch and wall'; and although it has not been fully excavated, Romano-British and possibly Iron Age pottery has been found here. Both hillocks are now graced with tall beech groves, known as the Wittenham Clumps, which, although they disguise somewhat the panoramic scene, do at least add a sense of mystery to this ancient place, and evoke thoughts of pagan gods and Druidical sacrifices.

Little Wittenham (or Abbot's Wittenham) consists of a small group of houses nestling close to a church (St Peter's). The tower is fourteenth to fifteenth century, though the rest is of 1863. At the west end has been placed a memorial to Sir William Dunch and his wife, who was sister-in-law to John Hampden and aunt to Oliver Cromwell. She touchingly mourns her husband with the words 'Tis for others too I put this stone: To me thy tomb shall be my heart alone.'

From here we cross the Thames by a footbridge 100 m downstream from Day's Lock, leaving the malmstone (a sandrock of the Upper Greensand stratum) on which we have walked since Wallingford, and passing on to the alluvial pebbles of the low-lying land around the Thames. Very soon we enter the line of the Dyke

Hills. The significance of these defences is that they protected the promontory of some 114 acres of land here formed by the Thames on two sides and the river Thame (which joins the Thames $\frac{3}{4}$ mile downstream from our bridge) on the third side. It is thought that they date from the Iron Age. Obviously, they were part of the same defence-complex as the fort on Castle Hill. They comprise a double line of banks with an intervening ditch. Originally the banks, then much larger than now, would have been surmounted by wooden palisades; and the large enclosure thus protected would have comprised a town-settlement and doubtless an area into which livestock could be herded.

After passing through and then along the outside of the earthworks we come in sight of the houses of Dorchester. But before we reach them we must advance our story of the past. For when the Romans came they built their own fort (Dorcina Castra), from which the present town is descended: and the traces of their fourteen-acre rectangular strong-point lie largely under the existing dwellings. From the town has also been recovered an altar dedicated to Jupiter. Roman Dorchester was originally built as a staging post on the north-south trunk road we shall be walking along in Stage 13. Trade then followed the flag (or rather, the eagles), and it grew to be a local commercial centre. But by the fifth century the legions had left, and the English (or Saxon) tribesmen were building their huts amid the Roman ruins. And the Saxons in time made Dorchester one of their principal centres. Thus it was to Dorchester that St Birinus, a missionary from Rome following in the steps of St Augustine, came in 635, and in the waters of the Thame baptised Cynegils, the Saxon King of Wessex, and his followers. This momentous event greatly facilitated the spread of Christianity in England, and Dorchester became one of the most influential Christian centres, comparable to Canterbury and Winchester, with its own cathedral and bishopric – until the eleventh century when the bishop moved to Lincoln.

Primed with these historical reflections, we now enter Dorchester and walk up towards the abbey, passing on the way a small Roman Catholic church dedicated to St Birinus, and the side of the causeway leading across the Thame. The abbey church of St Peter and St Paul was originally built in the twelfth century for the

Augustinian foundation which replaced the Saxon cathedral, and it is a treasure-house of medieval architecture and sculpture. The initial impact is not very striking: a rather squat seventeenth-century tower and unadorned exterior; and inside the church, a confusing moment when entering by the south aisle with its blocking wall halfway along. But once we have understood the basic divisions within the church we can appreciate its majestic grandeur in both aisles and in the full 56 m length of the nave, choir and sanctuary, each of different periods. The greatest glory is the sanctuary which contains three of the finest medieval windows in England. One of them (the Jesse window) is unique, the sculpted tracery designed as a tree growing from the seed of Jesse, and sprouting biblical figures, such as David: though the surmounting Virgin and Child were smashed by the Puritans. In the Lady Chapel are three splendid tombs with effigies, and that of the crusader Sir John Holcomb is astonishingly vivid. He seems to be about to get up from his tomb: let us hope it is to join a better world, though he looks suspiciously as though he wants to carry on fighting. Then there are wall-paintings, brasses, old glass, and other furnishings including a rare twelfth-century leaden font: and outside, a well-tended garden now surrounds this historic church.

Dorchester High Street is stiff with antique shops and inns. The George Inn is particularly attractive; timber framework with a jettied upper floor and a courtyard. It is of the Tudor period, and is thought to have been the abbey brewhouse at a time when the lives of some of the monks were scandalously lax. Anyway, there is no lack of refreshment here for those who have walked from Wallingford or beyond. As this is one of the shortest stages, those who have walked it only should not be suffering from sore feet. But a wide sweep of history haunts Stage 12, and all in all it has probably been the scene of more fighting and violence through the ages than any other of our Stages: indeed, at Long Wittenham near by hundreds of skeletons were recently discovered, thought to be the relics of some Saxon battle. So these ghosts may now need to be laid to rest in a pint of bitter at Dorchester before proceeding onwards.

Dorchester Abbey, south front

SPECIFICS

This Stage links Dorchester to Sandford across the flat Oxfordshire plain, broken only by the slight rise at Toot Baldon. Although the gravel-pits and council estate at one end and the electricity pylons and municipal works at the other diminish the attractiveness of Stage 13, the going is good through all of them, on firm paths and farm tracks. The intervening section of unspoilt countryside through the Baldons can be very muddy and possibly obstructed by cattle wires. In all, only half a mile is on roads.

ROUTE OUTBOUND

From Dorchester Abbey to Sandford Church 7½ miles (12 km)

(a) From Dorchester Abbey to Toot Baldon 4 miles (7 km)
From Dorchester Abbey walk to the main road by the west gate of the churchyard, then almost immediately turn right into Queen Street. Go to the end of Queen Street and then ahead by a path beside a cemetery. At a road turn right for 80 m, then left on to a signposted footpath which passes to the left of first a small gravel pond and later a larger gravel lake, after which it joins another path running between hedges. (When the Dorchester Bypass is constructed, the right of way will cross it near where is now the gravel lake.) Take this to the right, and then straight across a road and through the village of Berinsfield by way of a pedestrian path leading between the houses. Thence straight ahead on between fields. At a farm lane, turn 80 m right, and then left along a path between fields. Across a road and then on along a path between hedges marked as a bridleway. This path later broadens as a track. Ignoring turnings to left and right continue ahead to where the route degenerates into a rough path leading downhill, still between hedges, and crossing a muddy patch. It then veers left. At a house,

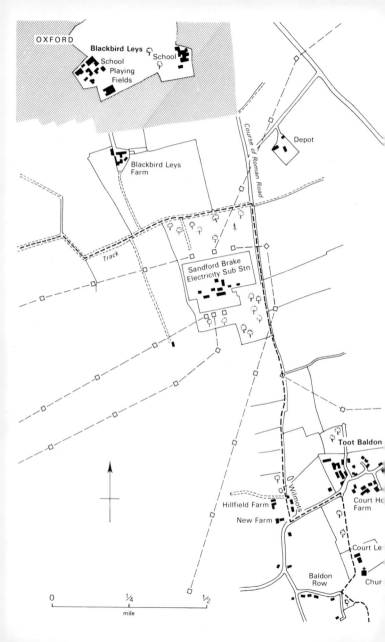

OXFORD

Blackbird Leys School
School Playing Fields

Depot

Course of Roman Road

Blackbird Leys Farm

Track

Sandford Brake Electricity Sub Stn

Toot Baldon

O Wilmots

Hillfield Farm

New Farm

Court Ho Farm

Court Le

Baldon Row

Chur

0   ¼   ½
mile

and the beginning of a small lane, turn up and sharp right along a path to Toot Baldon church, and thence by a driveway through a field to arrive at a road at the edge of Toot Baldon village.

(b) From Toot Baldon to Sandford Church 3½ miles (5 km)
At Toot Baldon, by the entrance to the driveway to the church, walk away from the village along the road towards Marsh Baldon for 300 m; then, just after a row of cottages (Wilmots), turn right along a farm track, passing close by a water-tower. Then down along the edge of fields, and at the base of the valley going past a pylon with a base platform. Thence ahead along a ride at the edge of a wood which soon becomes a tarmac road, passing the Cowley Electricity Station. Shortly after the station, a farm road turns up to the left, at the edge of Sandford Brake wood. Follow this farm road up and then down hill, following the direction of a line of pylons. This involves turning right on reaching lower ground and then shortly left, to keep in the same direction. The route then becomes a path, and leads immediately to the left of the Oxford Sewage Works. It then follows round to their main entrance, where we turn left along an access road which leads under the A423 road bridge. Then right into Sandford, and left into Church Road to Sandford church.

ROUTE INBOUND

From Sandford Church to Dorchester Abbey 7½ miles (12 km)

(a) From Sandford Church to Toot Baldon 3½ miles (5 km)
From Sandford Church turn left into Church Road, then right into Henley Road. Left under the A423 road bridge, then ahead at a sign for Oxford Sewage Works. After passing a caravan site on the right, turn right before the front gates of the sewage works and follow a path along the perimeter fence, turning left after 250 m. Where the fence turns left yet again, continue straight ahead to lower ground and cross a stream by a bridge on a farm road. Soon after, the farm road veers right and then left, proceeding parallel with a line of pylons, up a hill and then ahead down past the edge of Sandford Brake wood. At a tarmac road turn right, and past the entrance to

the Cowley Electricity Station. Where the road ends, continue straight ahead along the bridleway on a ride near the edge of the wood. Where the wood ends, continue on along the edge of fields in the same direction, passing by a pylon with a base platform. Then uphill towards a water-tower and past a row of cottages (Wilmots) to a road. Here turn left for 300 m to the entrance to a drive on the right, at the edge of the village of Toot Baldon.

(b) Toot Baldon to Dorchester Abbey 4 miles (7 km)
Walk along the driveway to the church, which leads through a field along an avenue of chestnuts. This leads to Toot Baldon church. Here proceed downhill and half right along a path. On reaching tarmac by some houses, turn immediately sharp left on to a bridleway which initially is merely a rough path between hedges and crosses a very muddy patch. Then up and ahead, where the bridleway soon improves into a farm track. Rejecting tracks to left and right, continue ahead to where the track gets rough again and straight on to the B4015 road by Little Baldon Farm. Cross this road and continue at a bridleway sign on a path through fields. Then, at a farm lane, right for 80 m and then left. The bridleway then continues between fields and then straight ahead through the village of Berinsfield, along a concrete pavement. Then, after crossing a road, it continues in a lane between hedges, with a large gravel pit to the left. Where the gravel lake ends, turn left to walk along the edge of it. $\frac{1}{4}$ mile later, turn right and away from the lake into a lane which leads to a road. (When the Dorchester Bypass is constructed, the right-of-way will cross it near where the gravel lake is now.) Go 80 m right, then left just pass the cemetery to a path which leads into Queen Street. At the end, turn left to the gate of Dorchester Abbey.

Approach Dorchester-on-Thames is 8 miles south of Oxford, and Sandford-on-Thames is 1 mile south of the Oxford ring road; and both are on the A423. Toot Baldon is a small village off the A423.
Parking Dorchester: Bridge End. At Toot Baldon and Sandford, in

village streets.   **Taxis** Didcot: Harold's Cars (tel. 814321).
Abingdon: Brian's Taxis (tel. 24780). Oxford: Radio Taxis
(tel. 49743).

APPROACH BY PUBLIC TRANSPORT

Trains (British Rail stations at Didcot, 7 miles from Dorchester;
and Oxford, 4 miles from Sandford.)   **Buses** Oxford South Midland
at Dorchester (War Memorial), Berinsfield (Turn), and Sandford
(Catherine Wheel).

PUBLIC TRANSPORT FROM END OF STAGE 13

To start of Stage 13 Oxford South Midland from Sandford to
Dorchester (half-hourly, once every two hours on Sundays: journey
time 15 minutes).   **To start of Stage 12** Same as above, to
Wallingford (journey time 40 minutes).   **To start of Stages 11 and
10** No convenient public transport, but possible by connection at
Dorchester or Wallingford to other Oxford South Midland services
to Nettlebed and Henley respectively.

ACCOMMODATION

Hotels Dorchester: the White Hart (Oxford 340074) and the George
(Oxford 340404).   **Guest House and Camping** Temple Farm
Country Club, Sandford-on-Thames (Oxford 779359).

REFRESHMENT

Pubs The Fleur de Lys, Dorchester: the Crown, Toot Baldon: the
King's Arms, Sandford-on-Thames.

DESCRIPTION

Now fame had through this isle divulged in every ear,
The long-expected day of marriage to be near,
That Isis, Cotswold's heir, long woo'd was lastly won,
And instantly should wed with Thame, old Chiltern's son.
And now that woodman's wife, the mother of the flood,
The rich and goodly vale of Aylesbury, that stood
So much upon her Thame, was busied in her bowers,
Preparing for her son, as many suits of flowers,
As Cotswold for the bride, his Isis, lately made;
Who for the lovely Thame, her bridegroom, only stayed.

Michael Drayton (1563–1631)
from *Polyolbion*

From the garden of Dorchester Abbey can be seen between the
willows the river Thame, which joins the Thames $\frac{3}{4}$ mile
downstream. Although the Thame is pronounced like 'name' and
the Thames like 'hems', only a little 's' distinguishes them in print.
This in itself ought not to have caused confusion (after all, France
has La Loire and Le Loire): but confusion the scholars of Oxford
certainly succeeded in creating. Noting that the formal Latin name
for Thames is *Thamesis*, they quite falsely assumed that this derived
from the river Thame and its conjunction with a hypothetical river
called the 'Isis'. This bogus theory thus provided the Thames above
the Thame with the alternative name of Isis – indeed an inauspicious
example for us of the fruits of etymology and geography as we
approach the university city! Anyway, Stage 13 starts by the Thame
('old Chiltern's son') and ends by the Thames ('Cotswold's heir'),
cutting across the Oxfordshire countryside so as to avoid the big
loop of the Thames near Abingdon.

   Leaving Dorchester by the quiet backwater of Queen Street –
which ends in complete quiet by the cemetery – we next have to

Dorchester Abbey, the Jesse Window

negotiate our way past two twentieth-century creations. The first of
these is the new Dorchester bypass, flanked here by gravel workings.
At the time of writing, construction work has not begun, and it may
be that deviations from the route will be imposed. The second
modernity is Berinsfield, a completely new village named after St
Birinus. Although it is the product of a leading firm of British
architects, Berinsfield somehow appears as an opportunity missed,
and one feels that it fails in coherence and character. Certainly,
there is a central green, but shapeless and without any focal point:
and the state of the houses bears witness to council leases rather
than home-ownership. The church (of St Mary) is a simple stone
box. The quality of life in Berinsfield would be much improved by
massive tree planting – along the rows of houses and in groups in
the central green – and by higher standards in the disposal of litter.

Our route through Berinsfield is by a straight path that lies at a
strange angle to the plan of houses and makes us somehow detached
from the drab architecture. For it is here that we pick up the line of
the Roman Road which we now follow – along or close beside – for
$4\frac{1}{4}$ miles. This is one of the earliest Roman Roads in Britain, and it
led from the Roman town of Silchester (in Berkshire) northwards
through Dorchester and on to Alchester (near Bicester in north
Oxfordshire). It was driven in a basically straight line through
woodland, heath, marsh, hill and dale, though with some minor
curves or changes in direction. We have already noted one such near
the Sinodun Hills. Another small one occurs just past Berinsfield,
where we proceed in a gentle easterly loop across a field: it is
believed that here the Roman road swerved to avoid the stream and
wet ground to the west. The road was built on a raised mound (or
agger) of some 7 m wide, and was paved with stones throughout its
length, thus providing rapid transit for horsemen and footmen
alike. At some points the *agger* may still be discerned, but of the
paving there is none. Still, here is our physical link with Roman
Britain, and it is good to think that the former highway now serves
as a byway, leading us directly towards Oxford, and providing us
with a tentative link with a civilisation that in Britain anyway vanished
without any continuing influence.

Going further back in time, archaeologists have been busy in the
area just north of Dorchester and around Berinsfield and have

discovered the lines of a Stone Age henge (a ceremonial circle, as at Stonehenge), as well as a *cursus* (two long parallel lines, 1,500 m long, between which tribal gatherings were held): and later in time at Berinsfield, a cemetery of the fifth-sixth centuries.

After crossing the B4015 at Little Baldon Farm our path deteriorates, and for a mile the going is distinctly rough and possibly obstructed by barbed-wire, despite the fact that it is here a bridleway. In this section we have left the gault earth of the beginning of the Stage and have entered the altogether earlier stratum of the Jurassic period (195–136 million years ago) which has produced clay. The clay around the Baldons is of a type called Portland Beds: around Sandford, it is Kimmeredge clay.

The Baldons – two little Oxfordshire villages – are rich in interest. They serve to typify for us the story of ordinary English country people through the centuries, on whose unremitting manual labour the whole edifice of culture, as expressed in palaces, colleges or churches depended. The first we pass is Marsh Baldon, although it is supposed that Toot Baldon, strategically situated on a small hill, was the earlier place of human habitation. Most of Marsh Baldon at the Norman Conquest was awarded to one Miles Crispin, and his holding there appears in Domesday Book thus: 'Geoffrey holds of Milo 10 hides in Baldedone. There is land for 5 ploughs. Now in demesne there are 2 ploughs, and 10 villeins with 6 borders have 5 ploughs. It was and is worth 100 shillings.' These villeins and borders worked for their lord and also held their own strips. Agricultural activity was grouped into three large fields, which alternated in the time-honoured triennial rotation of one year fallow for two years arable.

During the ensuing centuries there was a progressive tendency towards emancipation from personal allegiance and the establishment of powerful leaseholds, all of which weakened the original field-strip system. These social changes were manifested in the progressive enclosure of land into homogeneous fields, and this occurred mainly in the sixteenth and seventeenth centuries. This agricultural revolution was here associated particularly with Sir Christopher Willoughby, of Marsh Baldon House. This enlightened eighteenth-century gentleman farmed 400 acres. His flock of sheep was large enough for 80 to be slaughtered each year; and besides

this there were 19 dairy cows, together with poultry, game, dovecote and a fish pond; and arable land with wheat, oats and hops. Through the hedges to our left we can see the cottages of Marsh Baldon, and at a farm lane it is very worth while to deviate left for $\frac{1}{4}$ mile to see Marsh Baldon Green, still used for communal grazing, and, at the far end of the green St Peter's Church with its octagonal tower, and Sir Christopher's house beside it.

After Marsh Baldon, Toot Baldon. The tiny church of St Lawrence, which we pass, is situated in a remote corner, detached from the village. It got a mention in a bull of Pope Alexander III of 1163 – '*capella quae est in territorio monasterii in eadem villa de Baldindune*'. And much of the existing edifice dates from the thirteenth century. In the nineteenth century it was restored and reactivated by Oxford theologians who came here to preach and evangelise – a responsibility resulting from the fact that much of the village was owned by Queen's College. 'Toot' means 'look-out hill' in Anglo-Saxon: and, small though it is, Toot Baldon Hill ranks with those of Garsington and Headington as one of seven surrounding the University City. It is composed of a mixture of gravel, sand and clay, and is based on the surrounding subsoil of blue Oxfordshire clay. These geological features are reflected in the splendidly sonorous Anglo-Saxon names of the medieval fields of Toot Baldon – alderfurlong, yellowlandfurlong, redlandfurlong, thornfurlong, and wateriewergebed (willow-beds). From the church we walk along a drive flanked by chestnuts to gain the road, at which point if we went 100 m right we would come to the village of Toot Baldon, which contains some fine houses, especially Court House Farm and Manor House Farm, as well as the Crown pub.

After leaving the tarmac road and passing through a farmyard we come to the vantage-point – or 'toot' – and ought in theory to be able to spot the spires of the University City, $4\frac{1}{2}$ miles away. But instead we are presented with an extraordinary accumulation of electricity pylons, forming a weird wirescape superimposed on some pleasant agricultural land. The cause of these is soon apparent when, having negotiated some wateriewergebeds on the low-lying ground and a thornfurlong alongside Sandfordbrake wood, we pass

Marsh Baldon Green

the Central Electricity Generating Board's Cowley Main Substation. Shortly after this, we abandon the Roman Road (in this section known by the homely name of Blackberry Lane) and turn left up the edge of the wood. If instead of turning left we had turned right, a deviation of 1 mile would bring us by bridleway to Garsington, a charming village on a hill somewhat larger than that of Toot Baldon, and graced by St Mary's Church (thirteenth-century tower and chancel) and the Manor House, a fine sixteenth-century building which can be well seen from the road, flanked by enormous yew hedges in front and ilexes behind. It was at one time owned by Lady Ottoline Morrell, a formidable literary-lion-huntress who attracted the great names of Bloomsbury – notably J. M. Keynes, Lytton Strachey, Virginia Woolf and D. H. Lawrence – to the Manor House for weekend parties in the 1920s.

Meanwhile, our route across Blackbird Leys Farm is oppressed by pylons overhead and the brooding presence of industrial Oxford $\frac{1}{4}$ mile to our right. And worse is to come when, after crossing a small brook, our way leads around the municipal sewage works, past a depressing set of 'mobile homes' and then under the A423 bypass. But despite these unromantic concomitants this latter section of Stage 13 at least provides a traffic-free walk on good firm paths through basically agricultural land. Finally, we are rewarded on arrival at Sandford-on-Thames with a selection of pubs, and the sight of a pleasant broad street with stone houses, and then round the corner the church and the end of this Stage.

Of all the 16 Stages of the Walk, Stage 13 must admittedly be rated the least attractive, prosaically passing by contemporary utilitarian structures for more than a third of its course. But its useful function is to bring us straight across the countryside from Dorchester to Sandford, from Thame to Thames. And anyway, perhaps it is only right that we should briefly witness some of the realities of modern life, to put into perspective the monuments of the past, which can be done not only within Stage 13 itself, but principally within Stages 12 and 14, into which most of those covering Stage 13 will doubtless be extending their walks.

Toot Baldon Church

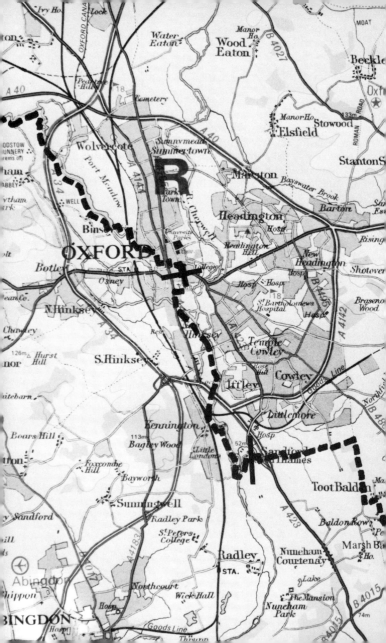

SPECIFICS

After leaving Sandford this short Stage leads for 3½ miles along the
Thames towpath in a rural setting, passing Iffley on the way, and
enters the historic centre of Oxford University through Christ
Church Meadow without any intervening suburbs. Only half a mile
is near traffic, and the route along the river bank is well gravelled
except for one short section.

ROUTE OUTBOUND

From Sandford Church to the University Church, Oxford 4½ miles
(7 km)

From Sandford Church go right down Church Road to the end, and
then past the King's Arms public house and cross the Thames by
Sandford Lock. Turn right up the towpath on the right bank of the
Thames (left as you look upstream), under a railway and a road
bridge, then past Iffley lock and, still along the towpath, to Folly
Bridge, where the towpath goes up to a road which crosses the
Thames. Cross the river by this bridge and continue along St
Aldate's for 300 m, then turn right into the Christ Church War
Memorial Garden, and then ahead into Christ Church Meadow. Pass
in front of the Meadow Buildings, then turn left along a path and
then a passage between Corpus Christi and Merton Colleges. Then
across Merton Street and up Magpie Lane and cross the High Street
to the University Church.

ROUTE INBOUND

From the University Church, Oxford, to Sandford Church 4½ miles
(7 km)

At the University Church cross the High Street and enter the
pedestrian passage Magpie Lane. Then cross Merton Street to a

passage leading into Christ Church Meadow. Where the wall on the
right ends, turn right and pass the Meadow Buildings of Christ
Church into the War Memorial Garden. At St Aldate's turn left and
cross Folly Bridge over the Thames. Then immediately left on to the
towpath on the right bank of the Thames. Continue along the
towpath past Iffley lock and later under a road bridge and a railway
bridge, and thence to Sandford Lock. Here cross over the lock and
walk past the King's Arms public house. Left at the road beyond
(Church Road) and up to Sandford church.

APPROACH BY CAR

Approach Oxford is 57 miles from London along the A40/M40.
Sandford-on-Thames is 1 mile south of the Oxford ring road, on the
A423. **Parking** At Sandford, in Church Road. In Oxford, St
Ebbe's car park. **Taxis** Oxford: Taxi Rank (tel. 42671); Radio
Taxis (tel. 49743); ABC Taxis (tel. 770681).

APPROACH BY PUBLIC TRANSPORT

Trains British Rail station at Oxford ($\frac{3}{4}$ mile from St Mary's
University Church). **Buses** Oxford South Midland at Oxford
(Gloucester Green or Cornmarket), and at Sandford (Catherine
Wheel). **Boats** Salter's Boats at Sandford and Oxford.

PUBLIC TRANSPORT FROM END OF STAGE 14

To start of Stage 14 Oxford South Midland bus from Oxford
(Gloucester Green) to Sandford (half-hourly, and once every two
hours on Sundays, journey time 15 minutes). Or Salter's Boats (daily
in summer, journey time 1 hour). **To start of Stages 13 and 12**
Same bus as above to Dorchester and Wallingford (journey time, 30
minutes and 1 hour respectively). **To start of Stage 11** No
convenient public transport. Nearest is Oxford South Midland bus
from Oxford (Gloucester Green) to Nettlebed, 2 miles from Stoke
Row (every 2 hours, journey time 1 hour).

1 Christ Church	7 Brasenose College	13 Schools Buildings
2 Corpus Christi College	8 All Souls College	14 Divinity School & Bodleian Library
3 Merton College	9 Queen's College	15 Sheldonian Theatre
4 Oriel College	10 New College	16 Old Clarendon Building
5 University College	11 Hertford College	
6 St Mary's University Church	12 Radcliffe Camera	

ACCOMMODATION

Hotels Oxford: Randolph Hotel, Beaumont Street (tel. 47481) and
several others. Iffley: Elms Hotel, Church Way (Oxford 778529).
Guest houses and small hotels Oxford: Nanford or Thorne Guest
Houses, Iffley Road (tel. 44743 or 40259), and several others. **Youth
hostel** Jack Straw's Lane, Oxford (tel. 62997). **Camping** (also
Guest House) Temple Farm Country Club, Sandford-on-Thames
(Oxford 779359).

REFRESHMENT

Restaurant The Mitre, High Street, Oxford. **Pubs** Sandford-on-
Thames: the King's Arms. Iffley: the Isis. Oxford: the Head of the
River, in St Aldate's.

TIMES OF ADMISSION

Parks and Gardens Christ Church Meadow daily 07.00 to dusk.
Botanic Gardens: weekdays 08.30–17.00, Sundays 10.00–12.00 and
14.00–18.00 (–16.30 in winter); closed Good Friday and Christmas
Day. **Houses and Museums** Oxford: see Stage 15.

FACILITIES

Tourist Information Oxford, St Aldate's (tel. 48707 or 49811).

DESCRIPTION

Towery city and branchy between towers;
Cuckoo-echoing, bell-swarmèd, lark-charmèd, rook-racked, river-
rounded;
The dapple-eared lily below thee; that country and town did
Once encounter in, here coped and poisèd powers.

Gerard Manley Hopkins, 1844–89
from 'Duns Scotus's Oxford'

At Sandford the brick, which has been the basic material for the
architecture so far along our route, begins to give way to the stone
that we encounter for the remainder of the walk, as we come closer
to the quarries of the Cotswolds. In and around Oxford the grander
buildings are of pure limestone ashlar, whilst the ordinary and more
modern houses are usually of a honey-coloured rubble stone known
as 'coral rag'.

   The church of St Andrew at Sandford-on-Thames is of eleventh-
century origin but mostly of nineteenth-century restoration.
Unusually, this restoration was undertaken in a Norman (or
Romanesque) style, and the tower is remarkably intricate in design:
but for the genuine article we must wait till we reach Iffley. The
seventeenth-century porch bears an inscription which could apply to
many of the churches on the Walk: 'Thanks to thy charitie,
religious dame, which found me old and made me new again.'

   On leaving Sandford church we very soon pass on our right the
Temple Country Club, where accommodation and camping are both
available. It is called Temple Farm because it is on the site of a
former preceptory of that militaristic and influential order, the
Knights Templar, who were given land here in 1240. Fragments of a
carving showing a Templars' cross have been found in the

Sandford: pub, mill, and lock

farmhouse. When the Templars were dissolved in 1312 the foundation passed to the Hospitallers; and then after the dissolution of the monasteries, to the Powell family. The Powells at least atoned for their windfall in that they remained steadfastly Roman Catholic through the ensuing centuries of religious strife, thereby debarring themselves from lucrative appointments, and at times facing persecution – the antithesis of the policy adopted by the cynical vicar of Bray in our Stage 7.

Church Lane leads us down to the Thames where a paper factory still occupies the site of the paper mill and where the lock provides us with a river crossing. To get to the lock we must pass in front of the King's Arms, on whose walls a notice proclaims 'This Land is Private: No Public Right of Way'. However, the owners of the public house are by this merely seeking to protect themselves in law against abuse and misuse and they do not at present prevent pedestrians from walking across their frontage and thence over the mill stream to the lock – and many people do so daily. In return for this permission, walkers of the Thames Valley Heritage Walk are recommended to call at the King's Arms for a drink and a snack, which if the weather is fine can be consumed in an adjoining garden on the river bank.

Here at Sandford lock we enter the orbit of the University, for the rest of this Stage is straight up the towpath to the 'dreaming spires' and (together with the first half of Stage 15) has for long been the haunt of Oxford men, on foot or on the river – 'cutting down swiftly, amid light breezes and pleasant sunshine, to Sandford, quaffing a cup of Mrs Davies' Anno Domini', as a guide of 1823 puts it. The daily walk, or 'constitutional', was an important feature in academic life, and often a stimulus to conversation or thought: '*ambulando cogitans*'. But I like the story of F. E. Smith, a brilliant undergraduate who later became Lord Chancellor of England, and who was invited for such a walk by a don whose custom was to let the undergraduate do all the talking, and then to demolish the young man's concepts with ruthless and sarcastic savagery. They began their walk in silence till the don said, 'They tell me you're very clever, Smith. Are you?' 'Yes,' replied Smith. For the remaining hour of the walk not a word passed between them!

Whether silent or talking we now will have left Sandford lock –

notable as having the greatest water-level fall of any Thames lock –
and started up the right bank. After 400 m we cross by a wooden
bridge a stream which leads to Sandford Weir, which can be
seen through a protective railing and is graced by an elegant
memorial to a student who was drowned in the pool below. The
1¾ miles from Sandford lock to Iffley lock is pleasant going, and
easy too, now that a raised path has recently been formed over the
water-meadows half-way along. We pass two college barges, at
present in derelict condition but destined for restoration; and, at a
steep bend, a picturesque house on an island. And then we go under
railway and road bridges, for half a mile distantly but not
obtrusively aware of cars, trains and pylons, and emerge in real
tranquillity at Iffley Lock. Before reaching it we can see on the
opposite bank the tower of Iffley church: and although from the
lock to the church is a ½ mile diversion, of all the short diversions
from the Walk given in this guide, this is the one I would most
recommend. For St Mary's Iffley is arguably the finest, and certainly
the most complete, Norman church in England. Even from the
outside it is apparent that we are looking at an entity of elaborate
sculpture, fashioned around the deeply recessed doors and windows;
and inside the effect of the three successive sections of nave, tower
and chancel, each with its variants of decorated arches and shafts, is
unforgettable. Even the adjoining rectory is basically twelfth-
thirteenth century, though its comparative simplicity only enhances
the glory of the church. (The church authorities have recently sold
this rectory, but fortunately it has been taken over by the Landmark
Trust, and from them is available for short leases.)

Iffley lock shares with Sandford the distinction of being the first
pound lock on the Thames, constructed (but since rebuilt) in 1635.
It also possesses rollers as an alternative for small craft to going
through the lock. From the balustraded bridge over the rollers, we
can get our first distant glimpse of the higher towers and spires of
Oxford University. We are approaching it by meadows and by
water much as people might have done centuries ago, and we have
successfully manoeuvred our way around the mass of modern
industrial Oxford, which envelops the old city to the south and east.
Only by experiencing its original segregation and distinctiveness, as
we are now about to do, can we readily appreciate the remarkable

history of how England's premier university, formed before 1200 in a place far removed from the king's court, grew progressively in influence, affluence and power to its apogee in the nineteenth century, all in its jewelled cluster of closely-packed buildings in half a square mile of land between Thames and Cherwell. By that time it had defied the last attempt at royal absolutism by James II and had utterly subdued the rival authority of civic Oxford – gown had triumphed over town – and through its University Courts, Senate and representation in Parliament had obtained special privileges which secured its independence. It was indeed the nearest that England ever got to producing a *polis*, or city-state, in the manner of Italy or Germany, or originally, of ancient Greece. But now all that real power and independence has gone, and only the outward form and fabric of it remain.

If it is term-time, and not too early in the morning, we will now see Oxford's oarsmen and oarswomen flexing their muscles as they pull themselves backwards on the water. There is a very wide variation in their skills. At the worst, a lurching, erratic, splashing, feathering effort: at the best, the Oxford eight in crisp, clean, confident harmony. We can both sympathise and admire. But the greatest fun for the spectator is to witness the bumping races – the Summer Eights in late May or early June (and the Torpids in March/April) – each over four days. In these, the College eights are stationed behind each other, and at the sound of a gun they all start rowing furiously to try and hit the boat ahead and score a 'bump'. The next day, the successful eights start at a higher position and the unsuccessful at a lower. The ultimate aim is to end the final day as 'head of the river'.

By this time we shall have crossed the stone bridge over a side channel and passed the University Boathouse. Here we can see the river Cherwell flowing in, on the other side of the Thames (or Isis). The land between the Cherwell and the Thames at this point is Christ Church Meadow ('rook-racked, river-rounded'), and beyond it we can now more clearly see some of the colleges. In the foreground are several college boat-houses, which replace the former twenty-two magnificent ceremonial college barges, of which sadly only one (that of St Catherine's) remains on site.

Eventually our towpath comes up to Folly Bridge where, on a

small island, we see Salter's boatyard (established 1858) and then, the other side of the road, an ornate red-brick house which here graces the entrance to Oxford. For the next 400 m we unfortunately have to endure the roar and rattle of a main road, albeit speed-controlled, along St Aldate's (a corruption of the 'Old Gate'). Compensation for this comes first from the Head of the River public house, with excellent pub food and a large balcony overlooking the river; and secondly from a good view up the hill ahead to Christ Church and Tom Tower, in which hangs Great Tom, the venerable bell taken from the former abbey of Osney nearby, which is tolled 101 times at five past nine each night, to call in the original 101 scholars. But thankfully we soon escape into the Christ Church memorial garden and thence into the meadow. A notice by the Magdalen entrance still proclaims uncompromisingly that 'the Meadow Keepers and Constables are hereby instructed to prevent the entrance into the meadow of all beggars and persons in ragged or very dirty clothes, persons of improper character or who are not decent in appearance and behaviour'. I only hope this will not apply to any holders of this guide-book.

Christ Church Meadow was very nearly destroyed when the local planning authority in the 1950s and 60s sought to drive a relief-road through it. But fortunately the University resisted to such good effect that the scheme was quashed. So we can still enjoy its fine conjunction of nature and architecture as we walk ahead along the broad walk (now denuded of elms), and pass the Christ Church Meadow Buildings (1866, Deane), a glorious achievement of High Victorian Gothic, now mellowing well behind ivy. At the point where we turn left we obtain a good view of four colleges. From the left, they are Christ Church, with the Meadow Buildings and then the spire of St Frideswide's, the cathedral of Oxford which is situated within Christ Church college. Then Corpus Christi; then Merton with its large square tower. And finally, further off and to the right Magdalen, from the top of whose graceful tower the choir annually sing their May morning hymn. Those wanting to deviate from the route by walking on through Christ Church Meadow towards Magdalen will be further rewarded by a visit to the Oxford Botanic Garden. This is the oldest botanic garden in Britain – far older than Kew – and was founded in 1621. In the original walled

area are two yews of the sixteenth century and, besides, a wealth of interesting plants both in the open and in the glass houses overlooking the Cherwell. We then enter the ancient centre of Oxford by a passageway between Corpus Christi and Merton.

J. S. Curl in *The Erosion of Oxford* writes: 'The whole fabric of central Oxford is, almost without exception, a wonderful amalgam of fine buildings, elegant spaces, grandeur, intimacy, superb vistas, glorious skylines and wonderful sculpted detail'; and I cannot better that description. In such a concentration of wonders, I can only select a few random aspects, associated with the buildings we can actually see as we walk through the middle of it.

For this we must at least pause at the point where we cross Merton Street. Looking to our right along this ancient street, the road cobbled and the houses gabled, we can easily imagine ourselves back in the Middle Ages. Immediately to our right is the huge bulk of Merton, whose large chapel dominates the residential quarters – built around 'quads', or courtyards; Oxford's oldest college, of thirteenth-century foundation, and hence appropriate as the first for us to look at. As such, we should particularly see Mob Quad (fourteenth-century) where the small-scale, intimate, enclosed, disciplined life of the medieval students is readily recaptured; and the chapel itself, with its magnificent thirteenth-century choir. The construction of this great chapel went on progressively until 1451, when the tower was finally completed.

Meanwhile immediately to our left lies Corpus Christi, an exquisite miniature college, exemplifying the spirit of the new learning of the sixteenth century, the small Front Quad adorned by a 'perpetual calendar', a sundial whose runes are incomprehensible to the uninitiated. Further on to the left we can see the Canterbury Gate into Christ Church, and a short deviation into the grandest Oxford college should not be missed, at least for those who do not know it well. From this back entrance we can progress through the eighteenth-century Canterbury and Peckwater quads (the latter with a great baroque library building along one side), and thence into the spacious magnificence of Cardinal Wolsey's original creation around Tom Quad, not forgetting the cathedral, so rich in Norman

Turner: Christ Church from the Meadows

decoration, the furnishings of subsequent centuries, and in religious and musical tradition (John Taverner was precentor under Wolsey). Christ Church has the further distinction of having been Charles I's palace for four years during the Civil War. His Queen held her court at Merton and cavaliers replaced undergraduates in the surrounding quads, and during the winter months – when campaigning ceased – music, masque and merriment helped them forget their predicament.

And so to the final few steps of Stage 14, up Magpie Lane past the back of Oriel, emerging into the High Street at a point where it starts its famous sweep (to our right), reminiscent of the curve of the Grand Canal in Venice, past All Souls and Queen's and down to Magdalen; a curve whose line is broken only by the solitary sycamore tree in All Souls' Warden's drive. In front is our destination, St Mary's, the University Church, its fourteenth-century spire dominating the scene, a marvellous elaboration of stone, with surrounding pinnacles and gables. Elaborate too is the church porch on this, its south side (1635, Nicholas Stone), a highly original design with twisted columns and classical motifs. And thus we enter the church where so many religious controversies have been dramatically spelt out – the trial of Cranmer, the new services of Laud, and the sermons of Newman, Keble and Wesley.

To complete our enjoyment of this culmination of Stage 14, we should by now have heard the bells of Oxford chiming the hours and quarters competitively, or ringing the changes in celebratory peal. Their sonorous tones provide a perpetual musical punctuation to daily life in the university, and they also bear a deeper message – for those that have ears to hear.

Merton Street

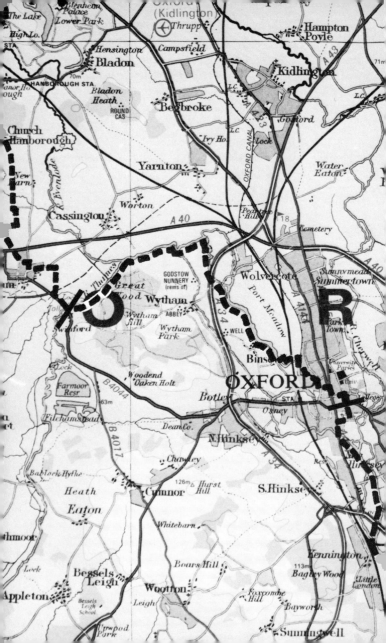

SPECIFICS

After a mile through the streets of Oxford, passing the University
Buildings and several colleges, the route leads across the edge of
Port Meadow and then, for all the rest of the Stage, along the bank
of the Thames, past Godstow and as far as Surnford Bridge. In the
first half as far as Godstow, the path is broad and easy: after
Godstow, whilst still well-defined, it becomes narrower.

ROUTE OUTBOUND

From the University Church, Oxford, to Swinford Bridge 7 miles
(11·5 km)

(a) From the University Church, Oxford, to Godstow Bridge
3½ miles (5·5 km)
From St Mary's Church walk up Catte Street past the Radcliffe
Camera and University Buildings, then left into Broad Street. At
end, turn right into St Giles' and then left into Beaumont Street.
Then right into Walton Street, left into Worcester Place, right into
Walton Lane, and left into Richmond Road, which leads into
Nelson Street. Then half right into Canal Street. On reaching a
small public garden at the end of the street, cross by footbridge over
the Oxford canal, then right and upstream along the towpath as far
as the next bridge. Here leave the towpath and take the small road
which leads left to the gate of Port Meadow. Continue ahead into
the meadow along the track, and cross the Thames at Medley. Then
follow the right bank of the Thames (left as you look upstream) all
the way up to Godstow lock and on to Godstow bridge.

(b) From Godstow bridge to Swinford bridge 3½ miles (6 km)
This is entirely up the right bank of the Thames (left as you look
upstream), leading at first under the A34 road bridge, then past
King's lock and later past Eynsham lock.

ROUTE INBOUND

From Swinford Bridge to the University Church, Oxford 7 miles
(11·5 km)

(a) From Swinford Bridge to Godstow Bridge 3½ miles (6 km)
At Swinford bridge cross to the right bank of the Thames. The route
then leads all the way downstream beside the river, going at first
past Eynsham lock, and later past King's lock, and finally under the
A34 road bridge, to Godstow bridge.

(b) From Godstow Bridge to the University Church, Oxford 3½ miles
(5·5 km)
Continue down the right bank of the Thames, past Godstow lock
and as far as Medley. Here take the footbridge across the
mainstream of the Thames to an island, and then another bridge to
reach the left bank. Through a gate, then ahead along a track across
the end of Port Meadow. After another gate and just before a road
bridge, descend from the road to the right on to the towpath of the
Oxford canal. Follow this downstream: then cross it by the first
footbridge and go through a small public garden and into Canal
Street on the right. Along Canal Street to its end. Then half left into
what is initially Nelson Street but becomes Richmond Road. Right
into Walton Lane; left into Worcester Place; right into Walton
Street; left into Beaumont Street. Across St Giles' and turn right
past the Martyrs' Memorial; then left into Broad Street. At end,
right into Catte Street and past the Radcliffe Camera to the
University Church.

APPROACH BY CAR

Approach Oxford is 57 miles from London on the A40/M40, and
Eynsham is 5 miles beyond Oxford, just off the A40. Godstow is
approached from the Wolvercote roundabout of the A40 and the
Oxford Woodstock Road. **Parking** Oxford: St Ebbe's car park.
Godstow: car park on edge of Port Meadow. Eynsham: by the
church, or at Swinford Bridge itself. **Taxis** Oxford: Taxi Rank
(tel. 42671); Radio Taxis (tel. 49743); ABC Taxis (tel. 770681).

APPROACH BY PUBLIC TRANSPORT

Trains British Rail Station at Oxford ($\frac{3}{4}$ mile from St Mary's University Church). **Buses** Oxford South Midland at Oxford (Gloucester Green or Cornmarket) and Eynsham Church ($\frac{3}{4}$ mile from Swinford bridge).

PUBLIC TRANSPORT FROM END OF STAGE 15

To start of Stage 15 Oxford South Midland bus from Eynsham to Oxford Cornmarket (half-hourly weekdays, once every 2 hours on Sundays: journey time 45 minutes). **To start of Stages 14, 13 and 12** As above, then Oxford South Midland bus from Oxford (Gloucester Green) to Sandford, Dorchester and Wallingford respectively (half-hourly, once every 2 hours on Sundays: journey times respectively 15 minutes, 30 minutes and 1 hour).

ACCOMMODATION

Hotels Oxford: the Randolph Hotel, Beaumont Street (tel. 47481) and several others. Wolvercote, near Godstow: the Oxford Europa Hotel (Oxford 59933). **Guest Houses and other Hotels** A wide selection, among them Town and Gown Apartments, Beaumont Street (tel. 48160) and Mrs Price, 338 Banbury Road (tel. 52076). **Group accommodation** St Edmund Hall, Oxford (tel. 48180). **Youth hostel** Jack Straw's Lane, Oxford (tel. 62997). **Camping** see Stage 16.

REFRESHMENT

Restaurant The Trout, Godstow. **Snacks** Many in Oxford. **Pubs** Oxford, Broad Street, the White Horse. Binsey, the Perch. Swinford, the Talbot.

TIMES OF ADMISSION

Houses and Museums Oxford: Schools' Quadrangle and the
Divinity School – usually open Monday–Friday 09.00–17.00 (–16.00
in winter) and Saturdays 09.00–12.30. Sheldonian Theatre: usually
open in summer daily 10.00–12.45 and 14.00–16.45, and in winter
12.00–12.45 and 14.00–15.45. Oxford Colleges' times of admission
vary and fluctuate, but generally they are mostly open in the
afternoons.

FACILITIES

Tourist information Oxford, St Aldate's (tel. 48707 or 49811).
Telephones Wolvercote, near Godstow: Eynsham.

Oxford Almanack for 1752: The Radcliffe Camera

DESCRIPTION

And, above Godstow Bridge, when hay-time's here
In June, and many a scythe in sunshine flames,
Men who through those wild fields of breezy grass
Where black-wing'd swallows haunt the glittering Thames,
To bathe in the abandon'd lasher pass,
Have often pass'd thee near
Sitting upon the river bank o'ergrown.

Matthew Arnold, 1822–88
from 'The Scholar Gipsy'

Emerging from the north door of St Mary's, the University Church,
or from the High Street into Catte Street, we pass by a sequence of
buildings whose variety and excellence provide a cynosure of
architecture as fine as any other in the world, and certainly
unrivalled in England. All that we see is made from stone – and
mostly from the lovely honey-coloured stone quarried from nearby
Taynton or Burford – supplemented only by the iron of gates or
railings and the lead of roofs or gutters. Even the humble cobbles or
flag-stones at our feet play their part in the ensemble, whose
essential secret is the use of scale and proportion, of intricacy and
subtlety.

    The central building in front of us is the Radcliffe Camera (1749,
James Gibbs), a library designed in the form of a rotunda or drum-
shaped building, with a dome reminiscent of St Peter's and other
Roman churches. To our left is Brazenose College, the gate tower of
1512 flanked by a façade mostly of the same date and graced with
three oriel windows. To our right is All Souls, the college without
undergraduates, whose annual election of two Fellows is the
ultimate accolade amongst those who have recently graduated with
full honours. The section of it nearest to us is fifteenth-century,
including the west front of the chapel: then beyond we see the low

screen (or protecting wall) of Hawksmoor's masterpiece, North
Quad, and can peep into it through a grille (though All Souls can of
course be properly visited through its entrance in the High Street)
and see the famous twin towers, which although built in 1733 are yet
in the Gothic style, brilliant precursors of all that was to follow a
century and more later. Completing this western façade of All Souls
is the frontage of the Codrington Library, in which Hawksmoor has
cleverly matched that of the chapel to disguise an essentially
different building.

Ahead of us, and beyond the Radcliffe Camera, is the Bodleian
library, through the arch of which we should now proceed – if it is
open: if not, pass ahead to the right along Catte Street. The Schools'
Quadrangle within is magnificent, with three pronounced and lofty
storeys bearing large mullioned windows and surmounted by
battlements. A tall doorway on the west side leads to the library and
the Divinity School; and opposite it, on the east side, is a
stupendous frontispiece of five storeys, with James I seated in state up
on the fourth level. Beyond the Schools' Quadrangle we next
observe the Clarendon Building (1715), also by Hawksmoor, but in
its somewhat heavy classicality very different from All Souls; and
next to it, the Sheldonian Theatre (1669), built by Christopher
Wren, and his first major work. Curved at one end, square at the
other, the perfection of it can only be appreciated by entering within
and seeing the rows and ranks of seats all beneath an immense flat
ceiling above which, amazingly, the bold cupola is supported.

Indeed all these famous University Buildings should be visited as
far as time and permission allows. In and around them we are
imbued by the spirit of the Renaissance; and hence even with the
ancient world of the Roman empire, whose Latin literature was here
so assiduously studied until very recent times. So it is not
inappropriate that we should leave them in passing by the sixteen
sculpted heads which look on to Broad Street and which are by
tradition referred to as the Roman Emperors. Of them Max
Beerbohm wrote, 'Here in Oxford, exposed eternally and inexorably
to heat and frost, to the four winds that lash them and the rains that
wear them away, they are expiating, in effigy, the abominations of
their pride and cruelty and lust. Who were lechers, they are now
without bodies; who were tyrants, they are crowned never but with

crowns of snow; who made themselves even with the gods, they are by American visitors frequently mistaken for the Twelve Apostles.'

Before going along Broad Street, a deviation of 150 m into Hollywell would bring us to the building of the Music Faculty, which has the distinction of being Europe's oldest concert hall, built for that purpose in 1748 and the scene of innumerable performances by great musicians. Concerts have also often been held in the Sheldonian Theatre itself, including a series of five given by Handel in 1733 and one by Haydn in 1791 when he conducted his Oxford Symphony.

We are now in Broad Street and despite the parked cars can appreciate the width which its name implies and which is due to its formerly being the space just outside the city walls. On our right Blackwell's, the university bookshop, and a group of old houses precede the railings through which we can see the seventeenth-century gate tower and chapel of Trinity to the other side of that college's large front garden. In complete contrast next comes Balliol, largely of nineteenth-century construction, especially in its Front Quad: and appropriately so, for under Benjamin Jowett (who was Master from 1870 to 1893) Balliol enjoyed the highest academic reputation, and many famous men received their education here, including those Edwardian men of power Asquith, Milner, Edward Grey and Curzon; also that last Edwardian, Harold Macmillan.

Set in the road in front of Balliol is a cross which commemorates the spot where Thomas Cranmer, the Archbishop of Canterbury who broke with Rome at Henry VIII's behest, was burnt by the Roman Catholic authorities in 1556 under Mary I. Just around the corner, after passing the church of St Mary Magdalene, we come to the memorial which was erected (1841, George Gilbert Scott) to commemorate the martyrdom of Cranmer and Bishops Ridley and Latimer.

At this point we enjoy a fine vista up St Giles' Street, longer and variably broader than Broad Street and lined with planes. The college buildings stretching up it to our right are those of St John's College. In Beaumont Street we first must acknowledge the Ashmolean Museum and Taylorian Institute (1845, C. R. Cockerell) built in the Grecian style. The Ashmolean is a museum of national importance, with a first-rate collection of paintings. For those who have trudged along most of the Walk the archaeological department may be of special interest, because it contains objects used by the early men who lived in Oxfordshire and at Berinsfield, Wittenham and Mongewell in particular. In sharp contrast to the Ashmolean, across the street stands the Randolph Hotel, a heavy Victorian Gothic structure. Beaumont Street with its fine stone terrace houses leads us towards Worcester, a college of special charm associated with its large garden which permeates right into the main quad: a college of eighteenth-century magnificence, but which also retains ranges of the fifteenth century.

With Worcester we leave the concentration of classical Oxford which we entered only $\frac{3}{4}$ mile before at Merton near the end of Stage 14. But before we actually leave the city we next pass through a quarter known as Jericho, which consists of small residential terrace buildings in streets whose names (Nelson, Wellington, Cardigan) indicate their dates. Obviously, as compared with Beaumont Street, these houses are of humble origin: but today, with compactness at a premium, they have become desirable residences, their texture, variety and intimacy in such contrast to the new council estates. Fortunately, whereas the walls of ancient Jericho crumbled at the blast of the trumpets of Joshua, this latter-day Jericho stood firm against the shrill cries of Professor Sharp who in the 1950s recommended the wholesale destruction of these 'slums', even though neighbouring St Ebbe's fell victim to the architects' folly.

To humble Jericho (thinly disguised as 'Beersheba') came – on foot – Jude the Obscure, Thomas Hardy's rustic hero. After attempting unsuccessfully to break through the class barriers and enter the university, 'he saw that his destiny lay not with these, but among the manual toilers in the shabby purlieu which he himself occupied, unrecognised as part of the city at all by its visitors and panegyrists, yet without whose denizens the hard readers could not read nor the high thinkers live'.

High above the small two-storey houses stands the tower of St Barnabas (1890, A. Blomfield). This is a most unusual English church, for the interior is of Italian Romanesque and thus ultimately Byzantine inspiration, with an apse at the east end, much gilt and many painted figures, an Anglo-Catholic shrine placed in a somewhat unreceptive parish. Finally, we leave Jericho and hence

Oxford by a pedestrian bridge over the Oxford canal, and then, negotiating our way betwixt railway, canal and iron-works, we come to the gate of Port Meadow.

Port Meadow is a large area of common land (in all, 439 acres) bordering the Thames, which from time immemorial has been held by the freemen of Oxford – a fact attested by a charter of Edward the Confessor. Nowadays the grazing rights are mostly acquired for horses and ponies, and scores of these keep the grass cropped very short indeed, especially at this southern end. The meadow is also pecked at by flocks of birds, in particular wild geese who like to gather in this watery haven. All the way up to Godstow from the further bank we look across to Port Meadow and can enjoy the pleasure – rare on the Walk – of seeing unenclosed land, and in this case enhanced by the towers and spires of Oxford beyond: though actually the ones which appear to us most prominent are not so much those of the old colleges as the parish churches of St Philip and St James and of St Barnabas, and the Oxford Observatory and the new Science Laboratories.

Meanwhile at Medley we rejoin and cross the Thames, and find a great conglomeration of boats around Bossom's boatyard: the family of this name held the toll rights at the nearby locks in the early nineteenth century and only gave up their control of the boatyard in 1960. Perhaps it was in one of their rowing boats that on 4 July 1862 two clerical gentlemen and three little girls went for a river expedition up to Godstow. One of them – Charles Dodgson – enlivened the proceedings by weaving a fantasy-story around one of the girls, Alice Liddell. The result was *Alice in Wonderland*:

> All in the golden afternoon full leisurely we glide
> For both our oars with little skill, by little arms are plied,
> While little hands make vain pretence our wanderings to guide.
> Anon, to sudden silence won, in fancy they pursue
> The dream-child moving through a land of wonders wild and new,
> In friendly chat with bird and beast – and half believe it true.

From Medley the remainder of this Stage is all up the right bank of the Thames. Half a mile upstream from Medley a bill-board proclaims the Perch at Binsey; and although the placement of

hoardings is rightly controlled rigorously in England (in laudable contrast to some other parts of Europe), I can forgive this one because the Perch is an excellent pub with wholesome pub food, which can also be consumed in the pleasant garden. The formula is very similar to that of the Trout, which we encounter just beyond Godstow lock. But the Trout suffers from its fame, as is indicated by the fact that its car park is larger than its garden, and often becomes impossibly crowded. At Binsey also is St Margaret's Chapel, with St Frideswide's holy well.

The river bank walk up towards Godstow goes past bushes, hedges and trees – notably several large poplars which bend gracefully over the water. By Godstow lock in a field are undulations which are thought to be the remains of a medieval field-strip system. After Godstow lock is passed, a ruin in a field ahead is all that remains of Godstow nunnery. Of all the medieval monastic foundations along the Walk, Godstow (which means God's Place) was undoubtedly the most aristocratic: indeed, Dame Ediva, who founded it in 1133, was called to establish it for twenty-four 'of the most gentlewomen ye can find'. It was heavily endowed by some of the leading Norman kings and lords, whose widows and unmarried womenfolk found here a pleasant and comfortable cloister from the rough hurly-burly of baronial life. Amongst them was Rosamund Clifford, the mistress of Henry II, when by pressure from his Queen Eleanor he was persuaded to part from her. She died here in 1176 and her shrine soon rather scandalously became a place of pilgrimage, until the bishop put a stop to such profanity. By the fifteenth century, standards in Godstow had definitely declined, so that the Church in 1433 had to issue an order that 'if any nuns admit men to feasts in their rooms they are to be excommunicated, for the scholars of Oxford say that they can have all kinds of good cheer [*omnimodas solaciones*] with the nuns to their hearts' desire' – which conjures up a pleasant image of Godstow as a sort of medieval women's college. In the Civil War, Godstow was garrisoned by the royalists and eventually burnt by General Fairfax in 1646.

After crossing a small road just before it bridges the river (with the Trout Inn on the further bank beyond an island from which we

Dawn on Port Meadow

may hear the sharp call of peacocks) we soon go under the Oxford ring-road and walk on up past some small river loops to King's lock, a recent addition to the lock system (1928). From here, the remainder of the Stage is different in several respects. First of all, it heads west and south of west. Secondly, the Thames is detectably smaller, especially above the confluence with the Evenlode, which occurs on the further bank halfway along; and also appreciably quieter, for fewer motor cruisers penetrate the upper Thames. And thirdly, the country is more rural, the towpath less frequented, and where Wytham Great Wood comes down to the river, the going is rather rougher. So here 'above Godstow bridge' is indeed the right place to evoke the spirit of the Scholar Gipsy as in Arnold's haunting poem, in which the elusive wanderer (or drop-out) is variously also seen in the Cumnor Hills to our left, and a few miles further upstream at Bablock Hythe. We may not see him, but we can perhaps appreciate his message since we ourselves are in a manner of speaking Scholar Gipsies as we pursue our quiet way past Oxford, temporarily abandoning our ordinary workaday lives for the slower pace of nature, and we too can get something of the mysterious feel of the countryside, especially if we are walking early or late in the day, or braving wintry weather 'while thick the snowflakes fall', or camping overnight near 'some sequester'd grange'. For myself, I must admit that I would like to compromise, and have the Scholar Gipsy as a companion on a long walk to Oxford, but at the end of the day to dine well amid 'drink and clatter' within the 'line of festal light in Christ Church hall'.

On the further bank we can detect the tower of Yarnton and the spire of Cassington; and then just after Eynsham lock comes Swinford Bridge, a worthy culmination of this Stage. For it is one of the most graceful Thames bridges, built in 1777, as striking and imposing as those of Richmond, Maidenhead or Henley downstream. With it we finally leave the Thames, which here has 43 miles upstream to its source at Thames Head Bridge and 118 miles downstream to London Bridge. An unusual relic of the past is the toll, and the toll-gate keeper has a comfortable lodge house built at one end of the bridge, from which he exacts a toll per wheel:

Swinford Bridge

pedestrians are not charged. Before the bridge was built, a curious annual ceremony was associated with the ferry. The parish of Cumnor (on our side and at that time within Berkshire) aberrationally extended into certain water-meadows on the further side (in Oxfordshire and otherwise in the parish of Eynsham). So as part of 'beating the bounds', the vicar of Cumnor would be formally received by the Swinford ferryman with a bowl of water and an offering of 6s. 8d., and then be transported to the Oxfordshire bank where he symbolically clutched at the reeds.

Eynsham is still one mile further by our route, but Stage 15 terminates at Swinford bridge because it seems a more natural boundary, and also because it is followed by a dreary $\frac{1}{4}$ mile along the B4044 road. But at the end of this is the Talbot public house, and then in Eynsham itself all main facilities are available.

The first half of this final Stage begins with a third of a mile of road
followed by half a mile of bridleway, before entering Eynsham.
After Eynsham, the section across the agricultural land of City
Farm can make for rather rougher going across fields. In the second
half, from Church Hanborough, the route is either on lanes or on
well-defined paths through fields, till it reaches Blenheim Park where
tarmac and earth-track alternate. Two and a half miles of Stage 16
are on streets or roads, but in other respects it is rural and remote,
and leads us up to a height of 114 m on the edge of the Cotswolds.

ROUTE OUTBOUND

From Swinford Bridge to the Triumphal Arch, Woodstock $8\frac{1}{2}$ miles
(13·5 km)

(a) From Swinford Bridge to Church Hanborough Church 4 miles
(6·5 km)
Cross Swinford bridge to the left bank of the Thames and continue
along the B4044 road for $\frac{1}{4}$ mile as far as the Talbot public house.
Just past the inn, turn right off the road and then right again on to
the track of a disused railway line which leads alongside industrial
buildings. After 150 m, turn right into a bridleway between fields.
This leads into Newland Street, Eynsham. At the end of Newland
Street, turn right into Hanborough Road, then left into Spare Acre
Lane, which bears right and later left. Where it bears left, leave it
and keep straight ahead on a bridleway which immediately crosses
the A40 road and then continues ahead between hedges for over
$\frac{1}{4}$ mile. At a point near an electric cable pole, turn right and
downhill along a path, still on the bridleway. After a further $\frac{1}{4}$ mile,
and soon after a footpath has gone off to the right, cross by a stile
to the left at a footpath sign, and go along the edge of a field as far
as a farm track. Turn left on to the track and then, very soon, right,

keeping the buildings of City Farm to the left. Continue on through a large field to its furthest corner, and then along the edge of a further field uphill to its upper apex. Then through a gate and along a track which leads along the edge of another field, with a hedge immediately to the right. This leads to a small lane into Church Hanborough. Where it joins a road at a corner, keep left and walk up to the church.

(b) From Church Hanborough Church to the Triumphal Arch, Woodstock 4½ miles (7 km)

From Church Hanborough church continue along the road which leads out of the village. At the end of the houses on the right of the road, and about 250 m from the church, take a footpath which leads half right through fields to Long Hanborough. At a road, turn left for 100 m. Then, opposite the Methodist church, turn right over a stone step and then a wooden stile, and walk down across fields to join a road at the bottom of the valley. Cross the river Evenlode and go under the railway bridge, and then straight ahead up the tarmac lane. Half a mile after the railway bridge, at a junction, take the right-hand lane as far as the Combe East End Gate entrance into Blenheim Park. Bear left along a tarmac park road to a point where it descends into a small valley. Before a cattle grid in the road, turn right and along a fence till a lake is reached, then continue along the lakeside keeping the lake to the right. Cross the lake by the Grand Bridge up to the front of Blenheim Palace. Turn left beside the park road which leads round by the lake to the Triumphal Arch into Woodstock.

ROUTE INBOUND

From the Triumphal Arch, Woodstock, to Swinford Bridge 8½ miles (13·5 km)

(a) From the Triumphal Arch, Woodstock, to Church Hanborough Church 4½ miles (7 km)

From the Triumphal Arch enter Blenheim Park and walk along the tarmac drive to the front gates of the palace. Here turn right and

away from the palace and cross the lake by the Grand Bridge. Then turn left on to a track which leads alongside the lake. Where the lake comes to an end, at the head of a narrow inlet, walk on away from the lake, then take a signposted footpath to a tarmac park drive. Turn left along this drive to leave Blenheim Park at the Combe East End Gate. Outside the park, turn right on to a small road for 300 m. Then turn left at a junction and on for $\frac{1}{2}$ mile to go under a railway bridge and then across the river Evenlode. Immediately after, take a footpath ahead and to the left of the road, which leads through fields and up into Long Hanborough. On reaching the village, turn left along the road for 100 m, then turn right up a signposted footpath through fields. Where this joins a road, turn left into Church Hanborough and so up to the church.

(b) From Church Hanborough Church to Swinford Bridge 4 miles (6·5 km)
At Church Hanborough church continue downhill into the village along the road until it bears sharply left. Here continue ahead up a small dead-end lane past houses and then on by a signposted footpath in a field, to the right of a hedge. At the end of the first field the path leads onwards to a gate at the top end of a large field. Keep downhill to the left-hand side of this field: then go through the middle of a further field, over some rough ground, and across a stream by a farm bridge and track past the buildings of City Farm. Just past the farm, turn left for 100 m along the farm road, then right by a signposted footpath along the edge of a field to a stile on to a bridleway. Here turn right and follow it for over $\frac{1}{4}$ mile up to higher ground. Near an electric cable pole, and between hedges, turn left, still on the bridleway, and walk down to cross the A40 road and into Eynsham, joining Spare Acre Lane, and following it around to the left. Turn right into Hanborough Road, then left into Newland Street. At the end of the village, where the road bears left, take a bridleway slightly to the right. This leads between fields to industrial buildings. Turn right just before them, along the track of a disused railway line. 150 m later, turn left and, by the Talbot public house, follow the B4044 road ahead for $\frac{1}{4}$ mile to Swinford bridge.

APPROACH BY CAR

Approach Eynsham is 5 miles west of Oxford, just off the A40.
Woodstock is 7 miles north of Oxford, on the A34. Church
Hanborough is approached by small roads from the A40 at Eynsham
or the A4095 at Long Hanborough. **Parking** At Eynsham and
Church Hanborough, by the church. At Woodstock, car park off
Hensington Road. **Taxis** Woodstock Taxis (tel. 812666).

APPROACH BY PUBLIC TRANSPORT

Trains British Rail halt at Combe Station (just by the crossing of
the Evenlode). **Buses** Oxford South Midland at Eynsham
(Church), Woodstock (Marlborough Arms), and very occasionally
at Church Hanborough and Long Hanborough.

PUBLIC TRANSPORT FROM END OF STAGE 16

To start of Stage 16 No convenient public transport. **To start of
Stage 15** Oxford South Midland bus from Woodstock to Oxford,
usually Cornmarket (half-hourly, hourly on Sundays, journey time
30 minutes). **To start of Stages 14 and 13** As above, then Oxford
South Midland bus from Oxford, Gloucester Green, to Sandford
and Dorchester respectively (half-hourly, once every 2 hours on
Sundays: journey times respectively 15 and 30 minutes).

ACCOMMODATION

Hotels Woodstock: the Bear (tel. 811511), the Dorchester Hotel
(tel. 812291), and others. **Guest houses and other hotels**
Woodstock: the Blenheim (tel. 811467); Tiffany's of Woodstock
(tel. 811751). **Camping** The Mill Caravan Park, Cassington
(Oxford 881490): $\frac{3}{4}$ mile from Eynsham and open April–October.

REFRESHMENT

Restaurant The Marlborough Arms, Woodstock. **Pubs** The Newland, Eynsham; the Hand and Shears, Church Hanborough; the Punch Bowl, Woodstock.

TIMES OF ADMISSION

Parks and Gardens Blenheim Great Park 09.00 to dusk; closed on one day in November or December: dogs on lead. Blenheim Gardens: as for the Palace. **Houses and Museums** Blenheim Palace: 11.30–17.00 mid-March to end October, including bank holidays. Oxfordshire County Museum: April–October, daily except Mondays.

FACILITIES

Telephone Church Hanborough.

DESCRIPTION

See, here's the grand approach,
That way is for his grace's coach;
There lies the bridge, and there the clock,
Observe the lion and the cock;
The spacious court, the colonnade,
And mind how wide the hall is made;
The chimneys are so well designed,
They never smoke in any wind.
The galleries contrived for walking,
The windows to retire and talk in;
The council chamber to debate
And all the rest are rooms of state.
'Thanks, sir,' cried I, ''tis very fine,
But where d'ye sleep, or where d'ye dine?
I find, by all you have been telling,
That 'tis a house, but not a dwelling.'

Anon. (? Abel Evans, 1679–1737)
'On Blenheim House'

In Stage 16 we strike north from the Thames to enter an area of low
limestone hills which are geologically extensions of the main line of
the Cotswolds, further west: but as far as Hanborough we remain
on Oxford clay, and the inclinations are only very slight. From
Swinford bridge we have to walk for $\frac{1}{4}$ mile along a fairly busy
country road before taking a loop through the fields by means of a
bridleway which in its initial section is on the line of a disused railway
– a common feature in England, and curiously similar to that of the
Roman roads: in both cases, a road network of prime importance
has become abandoned and is hidden in the countryside, discernible

Newland Street, Eynsham

only to those armed with detailed maps. By this means, we enter Eynsham along the raised walkways of Newland Street, past old houses of stone and brick, of which the most interesting is on the left, with three gables and fine brick chimney-stacks.

Those walking Stage 16 only may find it more convenient to start at Eynsham rather than at Swinford bridge; and if so, their starting point should be St Leonard's Church, which lies 300 m from our route and can be best approached by means of Queen Street which leads off Newland Street. This large parish church is mostly fifteenth-century and, with a big south aisle-separated from the nave by elegant columns, it gives a fine impression of space as achieved in the Perpendicular style. On the other side of the church is an area where formerly stood the Benedictine abbey of Eynsham, founded in 1005, in its day of comparable importance to the religious foundations at Abingdon or Wallingford downstream. Its first abbot was the great Anglo-Saxon scholar, Aelfric, who from his monastic haven made a vivid record of the turbulent events in England at the end of the first millennium. The church looks on to an irregular market square in which is a tall stone shaft: it is what remains of a medieval preaching cross, where the monks spoke on feast-days and special occasions.

Eynsham consists of two parts. As far as Hanborough Road the town is old; beyond it we come to new housing. But although Spare Acre is designed for modern car-bound life, the houses are pleasingly made of brick and with bright white woodwork and I award it the good marks I could not give to Berinsfield. Once across the A40 road and past a used car mart, our Walk leads through agricultural land towards Church Hanborough. The big fields (by English standards, at least) of City Farm are mainly used for cattle and horses. They lead us up to a vantage point where we get a good view backwards to the south over Eynsham and the Thames to Wytham Hill.

Church Hanborough crowns this small high-spot, and from afar we can see the tall spire associated with its name. Here is the most lovable of all the villages on our 107-mile route: houses and cottages grouped at every angle, protected by dry-stone walls and shaded by

Rooks circling Church Hanborough

trees. The church (of St Peter and St Paul) is magnificent, for not only does it have a wealth of early twelfth-century Norman decoration – notably in the north and south doorways – but it is a very complete and rich example of early fifteenth-century Perpendicular, with tall, slender, fluted columns in the nave arcade. Most impressive internally is the fifteenth-century rood screen, dividing the chancel and side chapels from the nave and aisles. That it survived the demolition of the Protestants is a testimonial to the comparative moderation of the English Reformation, which weakened in force towards the western parts of the country. The rood itself (the large wooden statue of Christ on the cross, flanked by the Virgin Mary and St John) was of course taken down and the stained-glass windows were destroyed: but the screen on which they stood, which was intended to preserve the sanctity of the chancel and the mystery of the mass, remains. Together with the fragments of stained glass and the Norman representation of the patron saint with his symbols including the cock which crowed twice, we can at Church Hanborough evoke something of the spirit of the unreformed Catholic church.

Long Hanborough, which follows after a short interlude, is less exquisite, and we only cut past the edge of it: though in it we will find some useful shops and pubs. Through Long Hanborough, in the small hours of 4 June 1644, came Charles I and the royalist army of 5,000 horsemen and 2,500 foot-soldiers on a forced march out of Oxford, covering 60 miles in three days. They passed this way, crossing the Evenlode a mile to the east at Folly Bridge, in order to slip between Parliamentarian forces at Eynsham and Woodstock, who threatened to encircle them.

The valley of the Evenlode is aesthetically somewhat marred by the railway-line driven along it but, that apart, it is particularly attractive and intimate, with the little river meandering through its grass banks and terraces. The gravels that have become exposed through the prehistoric action of the Evenlode have yielded important geological finds; and here at Long Hanborough have been found the bones of large mammals, including *Elephas antiquus* and *Rhinocerus leptorhinus*, whose appearance may stimulate our imagination. Anyway, we now cross the river – at the most westerly point in the whole Walk – and then walk up a country lane which,

though a public road, has very little traffic: from it we can discern
the tower of Combe church, and by this means we come to the
Combe Gate of Blenheim Park, for the final lap of this Stage and of
the whole Walk.

All this area was originally a primordial woodland which became
known as Wychwood Forest. It was to hunt in Wychwood Forest
that the medieval kings built their manor (or, as we would say,
hunting-lodge) at Woodstock; and here, as elsewhere, enshrined
their privileges in forest laws. Savage and restrictive though these
laws were, they did at least serve to preserve nature, and the land
around Combe would have resembled that which is described in
John Buchan's historical novel *The Blanket of the Dark*:

> Peter recognised his whereabouts. He was on the skirts of
> Wychwood, the other side from where he had dwelt as a child,
> and so to him unknown country. Away to the south he saw the
> lift of the Leafield ridge, and that gave him his bearings. All about
> them the forest flowed in a dark tide, so that it seemed to cover
> the whole visible earth. The little clearings round the hamlets were
> not seen, and the only open patches were the marshy stream-sides
> far below, which showed bright green among the dun and olive of
> the woods. It seemed a country as empty of man as when
> primeval beasts had trumpeted in the glades and wallowed in the
> sloughs. And yet their journey had been as stealthy as if enemies
> had lurked in every acre.

Anyway, whatever our personal opinion is about blood-sports, it
is certain that Blenheim Park owes its existence to them; and most of
our English kings from Ethelred to Charles II hunted here, regularly
or occasionally. As we see it now, it derives mostly from its
reconstitution after being presented to the Duke of Marlborough,
since when it has been primarily a place for pheasant-shooting
rather than stag-hunting. Not content with the plantations laid out
by Lancelot ('Capability') Brown for the fourth duke in the mid-
eighteenth century, the ninth duke in the early twentieth century
undertook a tremendous reafforestation and planted nearly half a
million trees in the 2,000 acre park, many of which we still see. Our
course through it leads through oaks and later beeches, and then we

come to the artificial lake created by Brown by the damming of the
river Glyme, and round a headland next can see the palace on
the opposite bank.

As we walk along the lakeside we pass 'Fair Rosamund's Well',
an ancient spring of water which is protected by stone surrounds
and an iron railing. Supposedly it was here that Henry II built a
bower for Rosamund Clifford (in the days before her banishment to
Godstow): but there is reason to suppose that the bower was in fact
created for his famous Queen, Eleanor of Aquitaine. She was a great
patroness of the troubadours and this secluded cloister, designed
around three pools on descending levels in the Mediterranean
manner, would have been a place where, like Marie Antoinette at
the Petit Trianon, she could escape from reality into fantasy; and
imagine herself as Yseult, with Tristan singing to her whilst the king
was out hunting.

And so we come up to a point where ahead of us is the Grand
Bridge over the lake, leading towards the palace. But before we
cross it, we should pause not merely to admire the vista ahead and
behind – whose elms recently fell to disease, and have been replaced
by young limes – but to recall that here formerly stood the manor of
Woodstock, before ever the palace was built; and, poignantly, such
ruins as did remain of it were dismantled for use in the grand bridge.
This manor was the scene of such dramatic circumstances as the
death of the Bishop of London in the arms of Henry I; of the love
of Henry II and Rosamund; of an assassination attempt on
Henry III; of Elizabeth I's girlhood imprisonment; and of a twenty-
day siege in the Civil War which, when the manor capitulated on
26 April 1646, signalled the surrender of Oxford and the flight of the
King. And Walter Scott, in his historical novel *Woodstock*, has
conjured up further scenes associated with Charles II's flight from
Worcester. But besides these dramas, it was more usually the scene
of the intimate domestic lives of many English kings, a place where
they were probably at their happiest; notably Edward III and his
numerous royal children, and Charles II and his numerous
illegitimate ones. But 'nothing beside remains', for all this is a
memory without a monument, other than an inscribed stone on a
plinth nearby.

Blenheim Palace from the lake

So without more ado we shall now cross the bridge and march towards Vanbrugh's baroque masterpiece, Blenheim Palace, the gift of Queen Anne and the nation to Marlborough for leading the allied armies to defeat the imperialistic ambitions of Louis XIV at the hard-fought battle on the upper Danube on 13 August 1704. It is England's counterpart to Versailles, and Vanbrugh himself regarded it 'much more as an intended monument of the Queen's glory than as a private habitation for the duke of Marlborough': hence the elegant criticism that ''tis a house but not a dwelling' has full justification. We have the satisfaction of walking up to it by the real 'grand approach', in contrast to the car and coach-borne crowds who are drawn towards it by lesser entrances. Behind us is the magnificent Column of Victory (designed by Lord Herbert and Roger Morris) with the statue of Marlborough (by Robert Pit) splendidly triumphant, inscribed with whole clauses of the Acts of Parliament which related his victories and endowed him with Blenheim together with all its 'franchises, customs, forfeitures, escheats, reliefs, heriots, fines, issues, amerciements, perquisites, and profits'. Under us now is the Grand Bridge (Vanbrugh) which straddles the lake in gargantuan fashion, and ahead is the Great Court where through an iron grille we can observe the massive door and portico with its elevated back-drop, the tall arcades, and the four square towers each surmounted by four tall finials – orbs with fiery plumes, which make impressionistic substitutes for statues. And on the left we can see the clock tower, on which are Grinling Gibbons' lions of England savaging the cocks of France.

Within, Blenheim Palace contains magnificent portraits, sumptuous furniture, and a series of glorious Flemish tapestries which were commissioned by Marlborough himself and depict fascinating details of his campaigns. Besides these there are the murals and painted ceiling of the Saloon, by Louis Laguerre, and an important collection of china. But most unforgettable is the sequence of state rooms in which these works of art are housed, the joint achievement of Vanbrugh and Nicholas Hawksmoor, starting with the enormous Great Hall with its vast interior arch, and culminating in the 55 m long library, which runs the full length of the west front of the palace. Beyond lie the water gardens in which the ninth duke and Achille Duchene sought to recapture the

Italianate formality which Vanbrugh and Henry Wise had envisaged but which had been swept away in the naturalistic landscaping of the eighteenth century. But to the south the grass lawn still perpetuates the aims of Capability Brown, and from the palace windows one can gaze uninterruptedly across nearly a mile of parkland to the tower of Bladon church, which is in direct axis with the grand approach and the column of Victory on the other side of the palace.

Bladon church (St Martin's) is the parish church of Blenheim, and has become a place of pilgrimage because it is here that Winston Churchill chose to be buried, next to his parents and in sight of his ancestral home. His genius provides a fitting culmination to the story of Blenheim: the great orator, the passionate politician, the Anglo-American statesman, appears in worthy contrast to his distant ancestor, the man of authority and few words, the intelligent courtier, the diplomatic general. Both of them stand decisively in history, and although Blenheim is artistically a monument to Marlborough, it is for us emotionally as closely linked to Winston Churchill. To reach his grave a deviation of 1 mile can be made through the lower park, by means of walking along the park road which leads from beside the palace to the Garden Centre: after the Garden Centre car park, take the next park road leading right, and then, after a cattle-grid, the left fork which leads to the Bladon Gate.

And so we reach the end of the Walk, around the bank of the lake. Here in the heart of the English countryside are complementary echoes of the scenes with which we began 107 miles back in Whitehall. In place of the relics of Whitehall Palace, here is a palatial entity. In place of the scene of the nadir of the Stuart dynasty, here is its apotheosis. In place of the tomb of one unknown soldier surrounded by many famous men, here sleeps Churchill surrounded by the forefathers of the hamlet. Here is Marlborough on his column rivalling Nelson. Here is a Great Court more impressive than Horse Guards Parade. Here is a spacious park, compared with which the mini-parks of London are cramped imitations. And here is an arch even more triumphal than that under which we started, and at which our Walk is now completed.

Beyond it a narrow lane between high walls leads us round into

Woodstock, and from the panoramas of Blenheim park we are suddenly transported into the intimacy of a small market town of stone buildings, several of them eighteenth-century or earlier. Fletcher's house contains the Oxfordshire county museum, well presented though somewhat educational, and with a geological section of special interest to long-distance walkers. St Mary Magdalen church is nineteenth-century with an eighteenth-century tower; its best feature is a Norman doorway on the south side, and it is worth walking past the church into the cemetery beyond to look at it. The eighteenth-century town hall is by William Chambers, originally with the ground floor open. And there are several hotels established in the Georgian houses around. Of these the best and the most well-known is the Bear; and for those who can afford it, the Bear provides the perfect place for meal or bed at the end or start of this Heritage Walk. In the words of Dr Johnson, when staying at Woodstock in 1776: 'Sir, there is nothing which has been yet contrived by man by which so much happiness is produced as by a good tavern or inn.'

In Woodstock, despite the ever-present tourists, we can feel ourselves very far removed from London. The town is in type like those of the Cotswolds – Chipping Norton, or Stow-on-the-Wold – and hence has links with the west of England. Certainly, we could spin back to Westminster in a car in only two hours; but in so doing we would see nothing and realise nothing. By contrast anyone who has walked the full 107 miles between Westminster and Woodstock will know very well that between the two lie countless gradations and subtleties, even though a common thread of history links them together.

(A) **Westminster to the City of London**

4 miles threading through the heart of London by means of gardens, alleys and small streets – $1\frac{1}{2}$ miles completely separated from traffic – mostly out of sight of large buildings and out of range of heavy traffic noise. The route leads to the Tower of London and passes directly by St Paul's Cathedral as well as seven churches (St Bride's, St Mary-le-Bow, St Stephen's, St Mary Woolnoth, St Clement's, St Mary-at-Hill, and St Dunstan's), and it goes through the precincts of the Inner Temple at times when it is open.

ROUTE OUTBOUND

From Horse Guards, Whitehall, to the Tower of London 4 miles (6·5 km)

From the Horse Guards cross Whitehall into Horse Guards Avenue. Just before reaching the Embankment, turn left into Embankment Gardens. Then across Northumberland Avenue and under Charing Cross Bridge into further Embankment Gardens. At end, along the Embankment under Waterloo Bridge and then left into Temple Place, reverting to a third section of Embankment Gardens from it. At the further end of Temple Place turn left into Milford Lane and then up steps into Essex Street. Right into New Court and thence into Inner Temple. (If Inner Temple is closed, go left into Devereux Court, then right into Fleet Street and right again into Old Mitre Court.) From New Court into Essex Court and then ahead into Pump Court and Tanfield Court, and then keep left to leave Inner Temple into Old Mitre Court. Then via Hare Place and past Serjeant's Inn, across Lombard Lane into Pleydell Street. Then left into Bouverie Street, right into Fleet Street, and right again into Whitefriars Street. Left into Hanging Sword Alley, then through Salisbury Square, and by Salisbury Court into St Bride's Avenue and across Bride Lane into Bride Court. Across New Bridge Street into Pilgrim Street. Right into Broadway and left into Carter Lane. At the end of Carter Lane, left across Cannon Street into St Paul's Gardens, then right across New Change into Watling Street. Left into Bread Street, then right across Bow Church Yard. Across Bow Lane into Well Court and thence into Pancras Lane. Across Queen Victoria Street into Bucklersbury, and thence into St Stephen's Row and on into Mansion House Place (rightwards): then left into St Swithin's Lane and across King William Street into Lombard Street. Right into Clement's Lane and left into Lombard Court. Across Gracechurch Street into Talbot Court. Across Eastcheap into Botolph Lane. Left into Botolph Alley and Church Cloisters and across St Mary-at-Hill into St Dunstan's Lane. Left into Idol Lane and right into St Dunstan's Alley. Right into Dunstan's Hill and left into Cross Lane. Then across the main road at Byward Street, and ahead into the continuation of Thames Street, which leads to the entrance to the Tower of London by Middle Tower.

ROUTE INBOUND

From the Tower of London to Horse Guards, Whitehall 4 miles
(6·5 km)

From the entrance to the Tower of London by Middle Tower, walk along Thames Street for 150 m: then, where it becomes a main road, cross it to the right and enter Cross Lane. At end, right into Dunstan's Hill and left into Dunstan's Alley. Left into Idol Lane and right into St Dunstan's Lane. Across St Mary-at-Hill into Church Cloisters and then Botolph Alley. Then right into Botolph Lane, and left into Eastcheap and immediately right into Talbot Court. Across Gracechurch Street into Lombard Court. Right into Clement's Lane and left into Lombard Street. At end, left across King William Street into St Swithin's Lane and right into Mansion House Place and left into St Stephen's Row and then Bucklersbury. Across Queen Victoria Street into Pancras Lane and Well Court; then across Bow Lane into Bow Church Yard. Left into Bread Street and right into Watling Street and across New Change to St Paul's Gardens. Then left across Cannon Street to Carter Lane; along Carter Lane to its end, then right into Broadway and left into Pilgrim Street. Across New Bridge Street into Bride Court. Across Bride Lane into St Bride's Avenue, following it leftwards and

around into Salisbury Court and Salisbury Square. Then into
Hanging Sword Alley and right into Whitefriars Street. Left into
Fleet Street and left again into Bouverie Street. Right into Pleydell
Street and then across Lombard Lane into Serjeant's Inn and on
into Old Mitre Court. Then into the Inner Temple. (If the Inner
Temple is closed, go from Old Mitre Court into Fleet Street, then
left along Fleet Street and left again into Devereux Court and then
New Court.) At the Inner Temple proceed to the right into Tanfield
Court; then Pump Court, Essex Court, and so to New Court. From
New Court, left into Essex Street and thence down steps by Milford
Lane into Temple Place. Then into Embankment Gardens and back
into Temple Place and along the Embankment under Waterloo
Bridge, and so back into further Embankment Gardens which lead
under Charing Cross Bridge. Then across Northumberland Avenue
into a third section of Embankment Gardens, turning right at end
into Horse Guards Avenue leading to Whitehall and Horse Guards.

(B) Woodstock to Ditchley Gate

2 miles through Blenheim Great Park, passing the line of the Oxfordshire Way.

ROUTE OUTBOUND

From the Triumphal Arch, Woodstock, to the Ditchley Gate 2 miles (3 km)

Leaving Woodstock by the Triumphal Arch into Blenheim Park, turn sharp right into the park and down a path which crosses the river Glyme and continues on past a cottage at the end of the lake. Continue ahead along a track which soon veers left and up to join the Grand Approach drive. Here turn right away from the Column of Victory and walk straight along the drive to the Ditchley Gate by the B4437, passing at a cattle-grid a point where the Oxfordshire Way crosses.

ROUTE INBOUND

From the Ditchley Gate to the Triumphal Arch, Woodstock 2 miles (3 km)

At the Ditchley Gate from the B4437 walk into Blenheim Park and straight ahead along the Grand Approach, crossing the line of the Oxfordshire Way at a cattle-grid. After 1 mile, and $\frac{1}{4}$ mile short of the Column of Victory, turn left down a track which leads to a cottage and thence to the left of the lake, crossing the river Glyme and emerging at the Triumphal Arch into Woodstock.

RAMBLERS' ASSOCIATION

The Ramblers' Association is the organisation for all those interested in preserving footpaths, obtaining public access to the countryside, and fighting for the rights of the walker. It is long established, has a large membership, and is organised through hundreds of local groups. Address: 1 Wandsworth Road, London SW8 (01-582 6878).

LONG DISTANCE WALKERS' ASSOCIATION

This organisation is for those interested in long-distance footpaths and other walks of at least 20 miles in length. It organises and helps a number of challenge walks where the object is usually to compete a set distance within a time limit. Address: 1 Lowry Drive, Marple Bridge, Stockport, Cheshire.

YOUTH HOSTELS' ASSOCIATION

This has over 250 hostels in England and Wales, of which seven are on our route. All hostels provide simple dormitory accommodation, but vary greatly in other ways. Membership is open to all. Address: Trevelyan House, 8 St Stephen's Hill, St Albans, Hertfordshire (St Albans 55215).

CAMPING CLUB OF GREAT BRITAIN AND NORTHERN IRELAND

The Camping Club looks after the interests of campers and has a number of sites, some owned by it, for its members' exclusive use, of which two are on our route. Visitors to Britain may claim temporary membership of the Camping Club and can use its sites if affiliated to the Federation Internationale de Camping et Caravaning, and holding a Carnet Internationale de Camping. Address: 11 Grosvenor Place, London SW1 (01-828 1012).

TOURIST ORGANISATIONS

British Tourist Authority 64 St James's Street, London SW1 (01-629 9191).
London Tourist Board 26 Grosvenor Gardens, London SW1 (01-730 0791).
Thames and Chilterns Tourist Board 8 Market Place, Abingdon, Oxfordshire (Abingdon 22711).

TRAVEL ENQUIRIES

British Rail Southern (01-928 5100); Western (01-387 7070).
London Transport including Green Line, (01-222 1234). **Other bus services** Victoria Coach Station, for Alder Valley and Oxford South Midland buses (01-730 0202); Oxford South Midland (Oxford 41149). **Boats** Westminster Passenger Services (01–730 4812); Turk's Boats (01-546 2434); Salter's Boats (Windsor 65832 and Oxford 43421).
Weather forecasts London area (01-246 8091); Thames Valley (01-246 8090).

COUNTRY CODE

All users of the countryside should observe the Country Code which is:

1   Guard against all risks of fire.
2   Fasten all gates.
3   Keep dogs under proper control.
4   Keep to paths across farmland.
5   Avoid damaging fences, hedges and walls.
6   Leave no litter.
7   Safeguard water supplies.
8   Protect wild life, wild plants and trees.
9   Go carefully on country roads.
10   Respect the life of the countryside.

The place names along the route are nearly all of English origin and mostly based on the principal English habitation-names of *tūn* (hence ton or town), a large village; *stoc* (hence stoke), a hamlet; *byrig* (hence borough or bury), a fortified village; *wīc* (hence wick), a village or farm; *stōw* (hence stow), a small monastic village: and on the English landscape-names of *ēg* (hence ey), large, dry ground by water, or island; *hamm* (hence ham), dry ground in the bend of a river; *denu* (hence den), a valley; *lēah* (hence lea), a forest clearing; *wiodu* (hence wood), a forest; *dun* (hence down), an upland; and *feld* (hence field), a cleared forest; as well as the familiar modern words and meanings of ford, bridge, ridge, cliff and marsh.

So, by combination we get such names as Eton (village on dry ground by water), and Woodstock (hamlet in the forest), as well as Aston (ash-tree village) and the more obscure Hampton and Hanborough (both high villages) and Cassington (watercress village). But the purely descriptive landscape-names are perhaps the most attractive, such as Cookham (high dry ground), Remenham (dry ground by the river bank), Cliveden (valley by the cliffs), Witheridge (willow ridge), Brightwell (bright stream), Garsington (originally Garsingden, a grassy down), Henley and Hurley (high and corner clearings), and, best of all, Iffley (plover clearing) and Dorney (dry ground of bumblebees).

A number of the names have personal names as prefixes, such as Ecga's, Byssel's and Witta's settlements on dry ground (Egham, Bisham and Wittenham), Sunna's village (Sunbury), Cerot's and Mul's settlements on dry ground (Chertsey and Molesey), Bealda's marsh (Marsh Baldon), and the maiden's – probably the Virgin Mary's – landing place (Maidenhead). And some have plural connotations, such as the village of Cynesige's people (Kensington). Of particular interest in this context is Walton, which means the village of the British (or Welsh) and hence implies that the British people continued to live here after the English invasions, possibly in free communities: and the same may be true of Wallingford.

Social activity is clearly stated in Hammersmith, Chiswick (cheese farm), Oxford and Swinford (fords for oxen and pigs), and

Rotherfield (clearing used for cattle): and the origin of Windsor may mean a landing-place with a winch. Religious establishment is discerned in Godstow (God's village, due to the nunnery there, and apparently the only place in England which expressly refers to the Almighty); and Westminster (the great church of the monastery to the west of London).

Older British names on our route survive only in rivers, such as the Wey and the Thames itself, which (together perhaps with the Thame) means 'dark river': except that also Bray means 'hill', and Dorchester derives from a British word 'dorcic', which may mean a bright place, and 'castra', denoting that it was a Roman town and of Latin origin. Of other languages we may note that Syon derives from the Hebrew Sion, Richmond from the French Richemont, and Blenheim is German. There are no Danish names, such as are so common in northern England, and it is merely a quirk that of all the 56 villages in England called Thorpe, the Thorpe on our route is the only one which is not clearly Danish.

Dates of reigns from 1066, with births, deaths and burials at points along the Thames Valley Heritage Walk.

House of Normandy William I, 1066–1087; William II, 1087–1100; Henry I, 1100–1135; Stephen, 1135–1154.

House of Plantagenet Henry II, 1154–1189; Richard I, 1189–1199 (born at Oxford); John, 1199–1216 (born at Oxford); Henry III, 1216–1272 (died and buried at Westminster); Edward I, 1272–1307 (born and buried at Westminster); Edward II, 1307–1327; Edward III, 1327–1377 (born at Windsor, died at Sheen, buried at Westminster); Richard II, 1377–1399 (buried at Westminster).

House of Lancaster Henry IV, 1399–1413 (died at Westminster); Henry V, 1413–1422 (buried at Westminster); Henry VI, 1422–1461 (born at Windsor, buried at Chertsey and re-buried at Windsor).

House of York Edward IV, 1461–1483 (buried at Windsor); Edward V, 1483 (born and buried at Westminster); Richard III, 1483–1485.

House of Tudor Henry VII, 1485–1509 (died at Richmond, buried at Westminster); Henry VIII, 1509–1547 (died at Westminster, buried at Windsor); Edward VI, 1547–1553 (born at Hampton Court, buried at Westminster); Mary I, 1553–1558 (died at St James's Palace, buried at Westminster); Elizabeth I, 1558–1603 (died at Richmond, buried at Westminster).

House of Stuart James I, 1603–1625 (buried at Westminster); Charles I, 1625–1649 (executed at Whitehall, buried at Windsor); Charles II, 1649–1685 (born at St James's Palace, died at Whitehall, buried at Westminster); James II, 1685–1688 (born at St James's Palace); William III, 1689–1702 and Mary II, 1689–1694 (Mary born at St James's Palace: both died at Kensington Palace, and are buried at Westminster); Anne 1702–1714 (died at Kensington Palace, buried at Westminster).

House of Hanover George I, 1714–1727; George II, 1727–1760 (died at Kensington Palace, buried at Westminster); George III, 1760–1820 (born at Norfolk House, St James's, died and buried at

Windsor); George IV, 1820–1830 (born at St James's, died and
buried at Windsor); William IV, 1830–1837 (born at Buckingham
Palace, died and buried at Windsor); Victoria, 1837–1901 (born at
Kensington Palace, buried at Frogmore, Windsor).

House of Saxe-Coburg Gotha Edward VII, 1901–1910 (born at
Buckingham Palace, buried at Windsor).

House of Windsor George V, 1910–1936 (born at Marlborough
House, buried at Windsor); Edward VIII, 1936 (born at White
Lodge, Richmond Park, buried at Windsor); George VI,
1936–1952 (buried at Windsor); Elizabeth II, 1952–.

Appendix 4 **Clock chimes and strikes**

Big Ben's famous Westminster Chime is echoed – at different pitches
– by Dorchester Abbey and by the tubular bells of St Barnabas'
Oxford; and was also echoed at Henley until one bell broke, and a
submediant was evidently substituted for the supertonic, giving a
most delightful and original effect. Merton and Magdalen both have
memorable chimes, in A flat and E major respectively, Merton
reminiscent of a Gregorian plainchant and Magdalen encompassing
(together with its strike) the full diapason. The chime of St Mary-le-
Bow is distinguished by covering a full octave. Eton and Horse
Guards have simpler 'click-clack' chimes, the latter with an
appropriately military rhythm; whilst Windsor contents itself with
only a single chime note. Other clock chimes exist along the route,
but are at present silenced due to lack of money for upkeep or
repair.